PRAISE FOR
Secret Confessions of a Wedding Planner

"As wedding professionals, we can say with certainty that this book provides a truly unique perspective. Allie has captured the heart of the wedding planning journey—both insightful and entertaining. *Secret Confessions of a Wedding Planner* is the perfect blend of practical wisdom and relatable humor."

MIRANDA AND WARREN CONERLY,
Warren Conerly Photography

"Pour a cup of coffee and dive in—*Secret Confessions of a Wedding Planner* is equal parts sass, humor, and sanity-saving wisdom. Allie Wester pulls back the veil with stories every bride will relate to and advice every mama will thank her for. Consider this your wedding planning bestie in book form."

TINA ELLENDER,
Senior Diamond Director, Bellame Beauty

"Allie Wester shares intimate behind-the-scenes secrets that will grip readers by the heartstrings and the funny bone while learning everything they need to know about planning a fabulous wedding."

PATTY AUBREY,
President of the Jack Canfield Training Group
and #1 *New York Times* bestselling author

Secret Confessions *of a*
WEDDING
PLANNER

A Behind-the-Scene Guide for Brides

Secret
Confessions
of a
WEDDING
PLANNER

A Behind-the-Scene Guide for Brides

ALLIE WESTER

ABUNDANCE
Alley
PRESS

To protect the privacy of individuals, some names and identifying details have been changed. Please note that the stories shared are drawn from my experience of them. Events may have been interpreted differently by others.

This book is intended as a guide to wedding planning. How plans are designed and implemented are ultimately beyond the author's control. The author/publisher is not liable to any party for any loss, damage, or disruption caused by following this guide, including errors or omissions whether such errors or omissions result from negligence, accident, or any other cause.

Published by Abundance Alley Press
979-8-9935506-0-2 - Paperback
979-8-9935506-1-9 - Hardcover
979-8-9935506-2-6 - eBook
979-8-9935506-3-3 - Audiobook

Dedicated to my children,
Briel JoAnne and John Michael.
I love you both with my whole heart and soul.

———————

TABLE OF CONTENTS

FOREWORD

I first crossed paths with Allie Wester ten years ago in Baton Rouge when she came to a signing for one of my books, *The Big White Book of Weddings*. She had an energy and presence that I immediately appreciated. Our paths have crossed several times since then at a variety of bridal shows and conferences.

In February 2019, Allie co-produced the Lafayette, Louisiana bridal show, Martini Masquerade, where I was the keynote speaker. The night before the event, we had dinner together. Allie arrived at the restaurant after working a wedding in Baton Rouge. She had slipped away from the wedding early to meet with me, leaving the bride and groom in the care of her trusted assistants. Just before Allie left, the bride had recorded a special video message for me and sent it along with Allie. Allie played the clip on her phone. Eyes dancing, surrounded by Allie and her bridesmaids, the gorgeous, happy bride announced that she was only releasing Allie from her wedding to me, and only to me. If Allie had been leaving to meet anyone else, she would not have let her go. It was a lovely clip, and the connection Allie and her bride shared was obvious.

At that moment, I knew Allie and I were kindred spirits. We both love life and the people we meet. We love celebrating. We love weddings and our brides, and we are passionate about helping our bridal couples celebrate their love with the most amazing weddings possible.

For Allie, that passion blossomed into the book you now hold in your hands, *Secret Confessions of a Wedding Planner: A Behind the Scenes Guide for Brides*. With twenty-five years of wedding and event planning under her belt, Allie has seen it all—the good, the bad, and the not-so-pretty. She is the event expert in South Louisiana. In addition to weddings, she organizes much larger events like Baton Rouge's annual street festival, Live after Five, which draws thousands of participants.

With refreshing candor, warmth, and delightful energy, Allie draws from all of her experiences and deposits them in these pages. She shares just about everything you need to know to prepare for the wedding planning process whether that wedding is for you or someone you love. You'll learn what to watch out for along the way, discover key planning details, and hear some intriguing stories—secret confessions—from behind the scenes.

Allie dreamed of becoming a wedding planner even before she knew such a profession existed. The path to her dreams wasn't easy. It isn't for any of us. Allie's journey resonates with me because I faced my own struggles along the way. Those struggles and a desire to help others navigate some of the ins and outs of the profession inspired me to create the David Tutera Wedding and Event Planning Experience, a symposium for event planners and designers. Allie channeled her yearning to guide others into the WBA School of Planning and Event Institute. To date, a thousand people have learned how to plan weddings and other events through that institute.

Why does she do it? She doesn't have to tell me; I know. Inspiring others is incredibly rewarding. It's just another way to share the love.

Life is beautiful. Every day is a reason to celebrate. This is never truer than when it comes to weddings. That's a vision I believe in, and it's one I know Allie shares. Secret Confessions of a Wedding Planner: A Behind the Scenes Guide for Brides makes it clear that Allie strives to ensure each bride feels like a guest at their own celebration and that everyone else who attends thoroughly enjoys each moment. That's why I support this book. Every bride should have the wedding of their dreams.

David Tutera

Los Angeles, California
July 2020

INTRODUCTION

Weddings are my life! I just celebrated twenty-five years of helping brides make their wedding dreams come true. It's a joyous calling this business of wedding planning, of helping a happy couple celebrate one of the peak moments in their lives.

I love weddings. I love my brides. I'm so grateful for my calling and the many ways social media has made it easy to stay in touch long after the wedding day has come and gone. I am blessed with the opportunity to watch my brides welcome new babies and to watch those kids grow. It's such a delight to share in their evolving lives!

Planning a wedding isn't as simple as writing out a "to-do" list and checking off the items, however. There are many moving parts to coordinate. From selecting venues and vendors to arranging for photographers and transportation, I ensure the bride's every need is taken care of, and I make sure people are in the right place and on time. Wedding preparations are often complicated by relationship challenges and intense emotions. It's my job to help brides and their grooms negotiate the whirlwind of feelings and responsibilities sure to arise as they prepare to say, "I do," and it's my responsibility to help them manage anything unexpected.

This book has been designed as a guide for brides. It shares numerous in-your-face truths that every bride needs to be aware of as she prepares for her wedding day. Sprinkled throughout these pages are secret confessions—stories emerging from my experiences as a wedding planner. Some are hilarious or even embarrassing. Others are simply eye-opening.

Although I primarily manage weddings in Southeast Louisiana, specifically in New Orleans, Baton Rouge, and the surrounding areas, I've planned weddings in Pennsylvania, Tennessee, Mississippi, Florida, and Texas. Experience has shown me that wedding traditions differ across the country. In larger cities like New York City, Los Angeles, Miami, Chicago, or Atlanta, wedding days are often long. After the ceremony, time is reserved for photography sessions and a cocktail hour followed by a sit-down dinner and three hours of dancing. Farther south a ceremony might last only thirty minutes followed by a three-hour buffet style reception.

Regardless of the traditions involved or the preferences of the bridal couple, common threads run throughout all wedding stories. All brides experience stress about planning details, from choosing venues for the ceremony and reception to selecting just the right menu and décor. And let's not forget the anxiety that goes with picking out the perfect wedding gown!

Relationships often prove challenging too. Weddings tend to bring out the best in people and the worst. They can trigger joy, love, and happiness, or jealousy, resentment, and contempt. Arm yourself with knowledge ahead of time, and bumpy relationships can be negotiated more easily. This book will help you do that.

Secret Confessions of a Wedding Planner makes it clear that you aren't alone in the process. You are not the only bride to deal with certain issues. This book will help you avoid many stress risks by making sure you're aware of the possibilities in advance. It is designed to provide you with insights, tips, advice about how to handle certain decisions and situations, and what to expect during preparations and on your wedding day. Moms, bridesmaids, vendors, wedding planners, wedding coordinators, wedding consultants, maybe even a groom or two, and anyone else who has an interest in weddings will enjoy and learn from this book.

The book is organized to help you manage the flow of wedding preparations in roughly the order they need to happen. I suggest you read it through sequentially first and then reread specific sections related to the task you're currently dealing with.

Have fun with the wide array of secret confessions! They're great examples of how unusual situations and circumstances tend to work themselves out. They should help reassure you that your day will work out too, no matter what pops up along the way.

My mission is to educate brides and their support teams about what to expect during the planning process and on their wedding day. I'm passionate about minimizing stress for brides. I want to eliminate wedding day surprises—you know, the bad kind—so no bride has to say, "I wish someone told me about that ahead of time."

If any of you have questions or concerns about your planning process or your wedding day, I'm here for you. Really. I'm here. You can email me at weddingsbyallie@yahoo.com or message me on Facebook, Instagram, Twitter, TikTok, or Snapchat at @ weddingsbyallie, and I will respond. I want your wedding journey to be fabulous because every bride deserves that.

A LOVE AFFAIR WITH WEDDINGS BEGINS

When I was a little girl, weddings were a huge part of my life. I attended loads of family weddings and loved every moment of them, from the fairytale splendor of ceremonies to tradition-filled receptions complete with dancing and loud celebration. However, I certainly didn't think about becoming a wedding planner. In fact, I don't recall any particular career objectives like teaching or practicing medicine or anything else. Yet here I am. I've been planning weddings for twenty-five years and loving every moment.

It's strange how your life's calling and purpose has its own way of finding you and keeping you on the right path. It's like a built-in global positioning device (GPS). The GPS sets your course and tells you where to go, but at some point you take a wrong turn or think a different way is better, and the machine announces in a small, tinny voice, "recalculating, recalculating!"

You take another wrong turn and it interjects again, "Recalculating, recalculating."

My life has been a series of recalculations. One of my first life recalculations took place in 1983. I drifted off course and got married at the tender age of twenty-three in my hometown, the small coal mining community of Hazelton, Pennsylvania. Although I've always loved weddings, I never planned to get married myself. My parents separated when I was nine. I wanted to spare myself the pain I associated with marriage. Two months after we got married, my husband and I moved to Baton Rouge, Louisiana. First, I found work as a leasing agent at an apartment complex, then in the mail room of a large Christian ministry.

MY FIRST WEDDING GIG

One of my mailroom coworkers, Debbie, was planning her wedding. The process fascinated me. Each day I asked questions about what she wanted for her wedding and how her plans were unfolding. At first, it seemed to be a futile conversation. Whenever I brought up ideas about dresses or cakes or photographers, she'd shut me down and tell me that there wasn't enough money for a fancy wedding. She and her fiancé were going to the Justice of the Peace for a civil ceremony. It was fine, she assured me.

Still, I couldn't escape the feeling that beneath her smiles and reassurances, she really wanted more.

I asked, "Debbie, if you did have the money, would you want a bigger wedding?"

"I don't have the money," she responded.

"But if you did, would you want more?"

"We don't have the money."

"I know but pretend you DID have the money. Would you want a bigger wedding?"

Finally, she confessed that she would.

That's all I needed to hear. I made phone calls to various vendors and friends on a quest to help make my coworker's wedding dream come true. Although I didn't make the connection at the time, planning her wedding tapped into my previous experience in the service industry. I had tried out all kinds of roles from waiting on tables and hostessing to food preparation and bartending. Managing a wedding reception is quite like working in a restaurant. I even taught myself calligraphy out of fascination with elegant script, a skill that sure comes in handy for preparing invitations.

Between those experiences and the many weddings I attended in my formative years, I probably always had the wedding planner gene. I just didn't know it at the time. I certainly never imagined I would make a living doing something so wonderful, or that I would eventually be invited to share what I had learned to help other people build wedding planning businesses too. What an honor!

I made great headway on Debbie's wedding. A friend donated bridesmaids dresses in a beautiful shade of cobalt blue. She included a flower girl dress constructed of the same fabric in yellow with a cobalt blue sash. A staff supervisor donated a gorgeous wedding gown with a matching veil. Another recently married friend shared her beautiful silk bouquets. Miraculously, the white, yellow-tinged blossoms coordinated perfectly with the bridesmaid's dresses.

I located a church that was willing to let Debbie hold her ceremony and reception there without charge. I ordered a cake for a steal of a deal from a local baker and served punch with it.

And finally, I found a pianist who agreed to play at the ceremony and reception for free.

Thanks to the generosity of numerous people, my coworker and friend enjoyed a simple but lovely wedding with about thirty guests in attendance. She was ecstatic!

So was I.

I can't begin to explain the wonderful feeling of accomplishment it gave me or the indescribable joy I felt by helping a dear couple celebrate one of the most special days of their lives. I was hooked. I wanted more.

After my first wedding gig, I helped friends and family members plan their nuptials. At the time, the official career of wedding planner didn't exist. I had no idea I could turn my passion into a real job. What I did know was that I loved every aspect of the process. From creating schedules for the wedding day and helping the bride and her entourage dress to coordinating the ceremony and reception, I loved it so much that I was doing it for free. The true key to living a good life, right? Find something you love to do so much that you'd do it for free and then figure out how to make money doing it.

That led to another "recalculating" moment.

INTO THE COLD

After moving to Baton Rouge and living there for about five years, I fell so deeply in love with the South that I couldn't imagine returning to the harsh, cold winters of Pennsylvania. However, even though I begged him not to, my husband took a position back in Hazleton. Reluctantly, I returned to Pennsylvania with him in 1989. Unfortunately, it was too much of a strain on our marriage. It ended just eleven months later.

I immediately moved back to Baton Rouge. Until I found my own apartment, I lived with old friends. I hoped the love I felt for the South would counteract nagging feelings of worthlessness and failure, but I had no purpose, no sense of direction. Even though I found work right away as a customer service representative with a communications company, I moved through my days like a zombie, numb and painfully lonely.

Loneliness led to another wrong turn, another "recalculating" moment.

I needed a car. In October 1991, I went to a familiar car dealership. I found a car alright, but I also found a handsome guy. Although the handsome guy wasn't the salesman who sold me a car, he asked for my number and we started a whirlwind relationship. Fast forward to April 1992. We eloped.

Deep down I knew jumping into another marriage was not the right thing to do. Red flags appeared everywhere with this guy. He was very controlling, possessive, and verbally abusive. But lonely and depressed people don't make the best decisions. I didn't listen to my GPS urging me to recalculate.

Only two months into my second marriage, we had a huge fight which resulted in a physical altercation. Low self-esteem led me to believe I deserved it, so I did nothing. A few months later, I discovered I was pregnant. Even though our relationship had continued to spiral, I was ecstatic. I never used birth control in my previous marriage, which had lasted five-and-a-half years. Because we never conceived, I thought I couldn't have children. But there I was, expecting a baby girl!

Despite my excitement—and the excitement of my parents—I still had a problem. I had to walk on eggshells around my husband. Any little thing would set him off.

BROKEN

I was eight months pregnant when my husband approached me with our check book, yelling about a mistake he had found. Before I could figure out what I'd done wrong, he struck me. My nose bled. This time he looked frightened. He immediately apologized and grabbed a towel to stop the bleeding. Looking back, I should have pressed charges or reacted more strongly to what happened, but I thought I loved him. Instead of taking action, I decided to forgive him and move on.

I showed up for work the next day with a black eye and an almost-broken nose. I told my coworkers that I fell on a stationary bike, but I could tell by the way they looked at me that they knew I was lying. I felt such shame, yet I stayed in that physically abusive marriage.

I can't speak for other women and why they stay, but I had several reasons. I felt unworthy of being loved. I felt stuck, as if I had nowhere else to go. I had no money, my car had died, and I was expecting a baby. I can honestly say that I am not that fearful person anymore. There is an old saying that your past does not define you, but I can say my past has made me stronger.

Once the baby was born things settled a down a bit. My parents came and stayed with us for several weeks. My husband never mistreated me when someone else was around, and I was far too embarrassed to tell them about the abuse. My parents had no idea about the trouble in my marriage until much later when I filed for divorce. When they learned the truth, they were crushed.

My GPS kept moving me forward even though I didn't realize it. When my daughter was about eighteen months old, I found a position as a church secretary where I could also coordinate ceremonies for all of the church weddings. It was there I received my first paycheck of $30 for doing what I loved and had already been doing for free. I was excited!

Then I found out I was pregnant again. Mixed emotions rushed through me. I was thrilled about the prospect of having another baby, but at the same time I felt wary about bringing another child into a toxic marriage. Five months into the pregnancy, my then husband decided to take a job at another car dealership in Boynton Beach, Florida. We would be near his relatives where we hoped to receive much needed help caring for the kids and the comfort of their presence around us.

A GLIMMER OF HOPE

Just before we moved, I learned about Weddings Beautiful, a school offering a home study program for wedding coordinators. I couldn't believe it. My passion for organizing weddings could lead to a legit career and training was available to help me get there! I immediately called their office.

The program required a twenty-dollar payment in advance of each assignment. There were twenty-five assignments in total. That amounted to $500. It seemed like a lot of money to me, especially since the move meant I no longer had a job and I was expecting another baby. I begged my husband to let me take the course. He told me it was a crazy idea. Wedding planning was a hobby that would never make any money. Despite his criticism, I was relentless. He finally agreed to let me do it—if I could find a way to pay for the assignments myself.

How in the world would I manage that pregnant, with a toddler, and without a car? My passion and desire to become a wedding coordinator was too strong to give up. That passion reminds me of a quote in the incredible book by Paulo Coelho, *The Alchemist*, "And when you want something, all the universe conspires in helping you to achieve it." The universe certainly conspired for me. Doors opened and opportunities appeared. I made money by babysitting and cleaning houses.

As I scrubbed toilets, I dreamed about being surrounded by beautiful brides, gorgeous flowers, and majestic cathedrals. That kept me going. Every two weeks or so, I'd send in my hard-earned twenty dollars for the next assignment. When the assignment arrived, I devoured it in minutes and quickly completed the work, but I'd have to wait another three or four weeks until I had enough money to send it back. It took me about two years to complete a course that most students finished in half a year. I'm sure my supervisors must have wondered what was taking me so long.

Living in beautiful Boynton Beach, Florida, should have been a dream for a beach bum like me. We were about a mile from the ocean and a gorgeous stretch of sand, but I only visited it once in the eleven months we lived there. I had two small children and no means of transportation. My husband only allowed me to borrow his SUV to go for groceries or to clean houses.

Our finances grew increasingly worse. When we moved to Boynton Beach, we didn't realize that the Florida car industry was exceptionally seasonal. Cars only sold in spring and summer. As the cooler months settled in, my husband was not selling cars and not making any money which put an added strain on our already explosive marriage. I didn't have a strong enough sense of self-worth to leave, and I was convinced I could never support myself or my children. I felt trapped and scared, so I stayed.

Eventually we moved back to Baton Rouge where my husband found a fantastic job as a finance manager at a car dealership, complete with salary, benefits, and commission. I was glad to go back because I had a wonderful group of friends there. Eventually, my husband even bought me an old beaten-up sedan because he was tired of lending me his car to take the kids to the doctor and run errands.

Unfortunately, our marriage continued to collapse.

DARKNESS BEFORE DAWN

Our fighting escalated when we returned to Baton Rouge. In fact, I even called the police a couple of times, but I never had the nerve to press charges. Even though he wasn't happy in the marriage either, he kept me in a state of terror.

Whenever I felt as though I couldn't handle things anymore, I phoned a pastor I knew, a friend and former teacher I really looked up to. He was a good listener, and he gave me some advice that I took to heart. He told me that in order to get out of the marriage safely, it would have to ultimately be my husband's idea. He thought my leaving would make my husband feel as though he'd lost control. That could create a dangerous situation for me and my kids. It made me think about those movies or documentaries where the woman in a controlling and abusive relationship tries to leave, so I grit my teeth and hung in.

Gradually, my husband began coming home later and later. Although that made things easier around the house, I worried about where he was. One Friday night he didn't come home at all. I was terrified that he had been in a car accident, that the kids and I would be left alone with nothing. I stayed up the entire night worrying, but there were no phone calls, no knocks on my door from the police.

That next day was Saturday. Saturdays are a huge sales day in the car industry. It was mandatory for everyone to be at work, so if my husband was alive and well, he'd be there. I dressed myself and my children—they were still babies at just two and four—and I took them to the dealership.

I walked into the break room at 9:00 a.m. to find all the salesmen sitting around drinking coffee. I asked if anyone had seen or heard from my husband. A few guys shook their heads. The rest scattered like roaches. Something was up. I returned home. At 10:00 a.m. my husband phoned and screamed at me. He told me to NEVER come to the dealership looking for him again. When I asked where he was all night, he said it was none of my business.

Not my business? I was his wife!

His reaction and his coworkers' reluctance to talk to me gave me the sneaky suspicion there was another woman in his life.

He came home for a few days, spewing tension in the air, explaining nothing. To avoid a heated confrontation, I knew not to ask any questions. On the Saturday following Thanksgiving, 1996—a week after I questioned his coworkers—he packed up his things and left. I don't remember what he said before he walked out the door, but I remember that moment like it was yesterday. I stood there, swept over by a tidal wave of emotions. We had a house, a mortgage, two small children, I was not working, and I was scared to death because I didn't know where my next dollar was going to come from, but all I could think was I'M FREE AT LAST!

I'm glad I listened to my pastor friend. Even though I was terrified about being on my own, my husband's decision to leave was one of the best days of my life. I no longer had to put up with a person who degraded me daily, intimidated me, and made me feel worthless. I no longer had to worry about whether my words or actions would set him off and trigger a physical attack. I was free. Truly free.

NEW BEGINNINGS

When my husband left, everything changed—and the best part is, it happened right away.   On Monday, two days after he left, I found a babysitter and hopped into my beater to drive around and drop off resumes at communications companies. I just happened to drive by the bridal shop, Classic Bride.

Should I dare try to go for my dream job as a wedding coordinator?

My inner GPS pinged, so I pulled up to the curb and stopped my car. My husband's words came back to me. *It's a stupid hobby and you'll never make any money doing that.* His words added fuel to my fire, and I stepped out of my car.

Sometimes proving someone wrong is the best motivator, isn't it?

TAKING THE BIG LEAP

As I opened the door to Classic Bride my heart was beating so hard that it nearly exploded from my chest. I took a deep breath and stepped into a shop that seemed to go on forever with pink walls. Beautiful bridal gowns hung everywhere. My dream world. Somehow, I managed to find my tongue and asked to speak to the owner.

I shoved out my hand. "Hi, I'm Allie Wester. Are you hiring?"

"We're always looking for sales consultants," the owner said.

"I'm also a wedding coordinator. I sell invitations and I know how to do calligraphy." Then, without giving the words time to register in my brain, another sentence popped out. "If you hire me today and let me book weddings through your store, I will give you half of my profits for the first year!"

What did I just say?

The owner's eyes widened, and her hand flew to her chest. "You're hired!" she said.

I couldn't believe it! I was hired to do something that I loved to do!

That first year, I booked twenty weddings and never looked back. Working in that little bridal shop changed the course of my life forever. It set me on track for my career and introduced me to a seamstress, Jeanne, who is my best friend to this day. I am truly thankful God allowed our paths to cross.

I worked at Classic Bride for ten years. The early years were full of struggle and constant growing pains for me and my business. Being a single mom, juggling work at the bridal shop full time, cleaning houses on Fridays, and spending Saturdays either working at the bridal shop or coordinating weddings was exhausting. But I was happy.

I was hustling all the time. I never took time off and was always trying to book weddings. I started volunteering at bridal trade shows because I couldn't afford to participate as a vendor. I would help other vendors set up, greet brides at the door, and then assist with cleanup—all to spend as much time as I could around brides.

Now I produce five of my very own bridal shows a year.

FROM VICTIM TO VICTOR

It took me a while to get over my divorce. I had to co-parent with my ex, and that meant I still had to deal with him and his intimidating ways. He always tried to put me down. He criticized my "stupid hobby" and frequently told me to "get a real job."

In the early days of our divorce, I probably played the victim card and used it an excuse for not moving forward. Mentally, I allowed him to hold me back in my personal life and my business. If you've ever had a relationship with someone who has constantly put you down and hurt you, you'll know how easy it is to question whether you're good enough or deserving enough to reach your dreams and goals.

That same sense of uncertainty and insecurity impacted the early days of my career as well.

When a bride asked me to plan her destination wedding in Santa Rosa, Florida on the same date I intended to be there on vacation, I declined. After all—vacation! She insisted she didn't need much of my time. I wouldn't have to assist with set up or break down, just coordinate the beach-side ceremony and get her down the proverbial aisle. Two hours tops.

Despite my reluctance, I agreed. I created a customized package formulated around her requests. I was to arrive at the site an hour before the ceremony, line up the bridal party, send them down the aisle, and stay thirty minutes after the ceremony to set her bustle to her wedding gown. And of course, I gave her a major discount.

Easy peasy. At least that was the plan.

When I arrived, the florist was still setting up. The mother of the bride shot me a weird look. I had no clue why. I lined everyone up and took care of the tasks the bride and I had agreed upon. I did not know that the bride had not informed her mother about the limited service arrangement we had negotiated for her wedding day.

After the ceremony, the bride's mother cornered me with disdain in her voice. "Why are you even here?" she demanded. "You have done nothing so far!" She continued to berate me.

I was stunned by her behavior. Because it was still early in my career and I lacked experience, I felt unsure about how to respond. All I could manage to say was, "I'm doing what the bride requested." My words were of no avail. I left that wedding feeling like a complete failure and cried the entire night. My vacation was ruined.

With all the experience I now have under my belt, I realize I should have stood up for myself. I should have shown the mother of the bride our contract and the low price I had given her daughter. She and her daughter obviously had different expectations.

Weeks after that fateful wedding, I received a bouquet of flowers from the bride's mother with an apology note. She was sorry for treating me badly. As I suspected, she had not known that her daughter and I had agreed on a limited amount of service.

I realized then that everyone who watches what I do or don't do at a wedding is judging my performance. While I'm not responsible for their attitudes, it's important to kindly and politely stand up for myself if incorrect assumptions are made. That was a major revelation for me. It caused an about-face in my GPS.

Another GPS recalculation occurred for me several years later when I read Jack Canfield's book *The Success Principles*. I came across a quote that really stood out to me: "You have to take 100% responsibility for everything you experience in life." I finally realized that ultimately, it had been my decision to start a relationship with my ex and my decision to stay in a toxic marriage.

When I took full responsibility for my life and stopped playing the victim, my life drastically changed for the better. I stopped complaining about how miserable my ex made me. I forgave him and forgave myself. I don't regret the marriage. Because of it, I have the two most precious beings in my life: my son and daughter.

I'm grateful for my struggles. They shaped me into the strong person I am today.

Because of my humble beginnings I don't take anything for granted. I strive to live in a grateful state and be aware of the many blessings around me. That attitude, combined with a lot of hard work and tenacity, has allowed my business to flourish. To date, I have helped more than a thousand brides plan their weddings. Through the school I created, the WBA School of Planning & Event Institute, I have trained more than a thousand students to become wedding and event planners.

Inspiring people to start their own businesses and watching them flourish is extremely fulfilling. Showing others that it's possible to live the life of your dreams—and teaching them how to do it—is incredibly special. I am honored and humbled by the lives that have changed as a result of my school.

The dream I had while cleaning toilets has come true. Now I'm surrounded by beautiful brides, gorgeous flowers, and majestic cathedrals almost every weekend. I have the opportunity to play a central role in one of life's peak moments with many couples.

If I can live my dream life, then so can you.

Secret Confession

LESSON LEARNED THE HARD WAY

This story is my own confession. It involves an event that took place when I was young and new to the wedding industry and a prayer that I'm pretty sure most people are familiar with: "Dear God, if you can get me through this, I will never, ever (fill in the blank) again."

When I began my career as a wedding coordinator, I worked for a successful wedding planner from New Orleans. This wedding planner—let's call her Mary—would sub-contract me and a few others to be her point people for weddings. She would show up at key moments, for instance right before the bride was about to go down the aisle or when she arrived at the reception. Quite brilliant.

One weekend, Mary subcontracted me for two weddings in New Orleans, each with a rehearsal on Friday night and the ceremony/reception the next day. My two children were young, and I was recently separated, so I hired a babysitter for the rehearsals. My ex-husband agreed to pick up them up for the day of the weddings.

The first rehearsal took place at one of the most famous Catholic Churches in the nation, the iconic, castle-like St. Louis Cathedral in Jackson Square, the French Quarter. After that was successfully tended to, I drove to the stately NOLA Museum of Art, nestled in the lush atmosphere of City Park where a bride and groom had planned a destination wedding.

To my surprise and delight, everyone at the rehearsal was from my home state, Pennsylvania. The entire bridal party were Penn State Alumni just like me! What a thrill! If you're so closely tied to your college football team that you bleed certain colors—in this case blue and white—you'll know what I'm talking about. After living in Louisiana for years, I felt like I'd found twenty long lost best friends.

They invited me to the rehearsal dinner at Pat O'Brien's on St. Peter Street and I accepted. As a wedding coordinator newbie, I was green to the protocol and professionalism of the field or I might have decided otherwise. I was also new to the beverage known as a "Hurricane." We had such a terrific time reminiscing about Penn State that I didn't notice how easily the intoxicating red cocktail went down.

When I rose to leave, my head spun a little. Otherwise I felt fine.

Waking up the next morning was another thing. Talk about a hangover! I stumbled to the bathroom and folded over the toilet bowl. Thankfully, my ex-husband came to pick up the kids. I was so queasy I could hardly move, but I managed to get dressed. Then I heaved again. For the hour-and-a-half drive from Baton Rouge to New Orleans I travelled in abject misery with a bowl between my legs, vomiting all the way. To top it off, the sky had opened up. It was "monsooning." Rain fell sideways in torrential buckets. I could barely see the road in front of me.

A sixteen-hour day lay ahead. With a desperate need for money, I couldn't call in sick. Instead, I began to pray. "Dear God, if you get me through this day I will never, ever, ever, ever drink the night before a wedding ever again. Amen."

When I finally crawled out of my car at the hotel where the bride was getting her hair and makeup done, a gust of wind blew my umbrella inside out. I got soaked. Perfect. Drenched from head to toe, looking like a drowned rat, and sick as a dog. Could the day get any worse?

Apparently, it could. The bride was in tears because of the weather. She feared the rain would cancel plans for a horse and open carriage in her second line parade from the ceremony to the reception. (See "Secret Confession: A Day in the Life," Chapter 2, for more about second line parades.) The makeup artist had to continually touch up her face to cover tear stains. I reminded her that Louisiana weather could change in minutes from stormy to sunny, and we left the schedule as planned.

When I arrived at St. Louis Cathedral for her ceremony, I was still sick. As my stomach threatened to heave again, I approached a Deacon.

"Excuse me," I managed. "Can you tell me where the restroom is?"

He looked me up and down with concern. "The church is extremely old. There are no restrooms. You'll have to go down the street to another venue."

I'm sure I turned green. Was he kidding me? I'd never make it! So, in the middle of torrential rains, I stepped into the alley outside of St. Louis Cathedral and threw up.

How mortifying.

Somehow, I managed to pull myself together when Mary dropped in for her appearance, and I was able to get the bridal party and the bride down the aisle without any problems. The second they said, "I do," sunlight streamed through the stained-glass windows of the church. It was one of those movie moments; I could almost hear the Hallelujah chorus. What a miracle!

The second line parade went as planned, complete with horse and open carriage.

I breathed a sigh of relief. There. One ceremony down, another ceremony and two receptions to go. But my nausea and dizziness continued, and I still had eleven hours of work ahead.

It wasn't until about 8:00 p.m. that I started feeling better and light began to glow at the end of the tunnel for this long, difficult, and humbling day. After my new Penn State friends had departed later that evening and I finished cleaning up the venue, I crawled into my car for the drive home to Baton Rouge, tired, aching, and relieved. I'd made it through one of the most difficult days of my life. I recalled my prayer: "Dear God, if you get me through these weddings today, I will never, ever, ever, ever drink the night before a wedding again. Ever."

And guess what? In the twenty-five years since, I never, ever have.

GETTING PROFESSIONAL HELP

M ention "the wedding planner," and people are immediately reminded of the 2001 movie starring Jennifer Lopez and Matthew McConaughey. That movie sure put wedding planners on the map! I'm forever grateful for the recognition and impact it's had on my life—even if life as a wedding planner isn't quite as glamourous as the movie makes it out to be. Unlike Jennifer Lopez's character, Mary Fiore, I've never fallen in love with one of my bride's grooms. (I am, however, still waiting for a Matthew McConaughey clone to save me from an oncoming truck!)

The movie brought wedding planning to the attention of a wider audience, and that boosted my business. It also launched numerous inquiries from people wanting to know how to become wedding planners. Those phone calls, bolstered by the encouragement I received from Tony Robbins' motivational CD series *Personal Power*, inspired me to create the WBA School of Planning & Event Institute to teach other people the ins and outs of wedding planning.

What a huge impact and blessing that movie has had on my life! Thank you, "Jenny from the block."

As I was driving home from a wedding recently at 1:00 a.m., tired, sore, and reflecting on the event, I realized what an oxymoron the role of wedding "planner" really is. The entire process of planning a wedding is full of contradictions and complications that are difficult to anticipate, which is exactly why brides need professional support. (It's also why wedding planning creates such exciting content for a movie.)

A great wedding planner must be thoroughly organized, yet flexible when plans and circumstances change because they always do. Making sure people show up on time and stick to the schedule requires a stern hand with a friendly, kind demeanor. That isn't always easy. Have you ever tried to round up twenty people in party mode for a photograph session? It's like herding cats!

Weddings have a way of bringing out the best and the absolute worst in people. As a referee, I've stopped arguments between the bride and her mother or mother-in-law to be. As a diplomat, I've often negotiated sensitive issues between the bride and her groom or family. As an ambassador, I've promoted requests on behalf of the bride and groom. As a therapist, I've listened to confessions from brides, moms, grooms, and even fathers of brides. Wedding circumstances are so emotional that some families could use a therapist to get through the whole occasion. With all the unexpected situations that can arise, a wedding planner needs the problem-solving skills of MacGyver, ready for anything at any time.

It helps to be a willing scapegoat too. If the bride has a difficult decision to make and is concerned she might hurt someone's feelings, I tell her to blame it on me. She must live with these people the rest of her life, but I do not.

On top of all those challenges, a dream wedding atmosphere is always required, but costs must fall within a given budget. Sometimes that takes a miracle worker.

WHY YOU (AND I) NEED A WEDDING PLANNER

I'm often asked if I will be the wedding planner for my daughter should she decide to get married one day. What a great question! When I started my wedding planning business, she was only four years old. Now she's lovely young woman of twenty-three. As I write this book, she isn't thinking about marriage—she's having a blast in college and living life to the fullest—but one day, a wedding may come.

I must admit, I do dream about the time when it will be her turn to walk down the aisle. We talk about it too. She dreams of a destination wedding out in the woods somewhere, or perhaps on a sunny island. But I won't plan her wedding. I'll hire someone else to do the job for me.

Why, you ask? Why would a professional wedding planner hire a wedding planner for her daughter's big day? Because just like the bride I'll have too many other things to focus on.

Even if you are the super organized type who has chosen venues and vendors and written out a minute by minute itinerary, you'll need someone else to manage the details on your wedding day. Trust me. You'll be preoccupied. As the bride you will be sequestered for a good part of the day to have your hair and makeup done and to get dressed. On top of that you'll be consumed by emotion and possibly a few jitters. More than likely your mother will be in the same boat. (I know I'll be riding the waves when my daughter gets married!)

If you and your mother are busy, who will see to it that the vendors arrive on time? Who will ensure your table décor and accessories are placed just as you envisioned them? Who will put out any fires that flare up? (Believe me, they will!) Who will round up your bridal party and get them to the church on time? Who will line up your processional and send it down the aisle to the correct music?

You get the picture. There's a lot to do and clearly you can't take care of those details when your stylist has a hot iron to your head. Neither can I! I want to enjoy my daughter's wedding day and leave the running around to someone else. You should do the same.

If you haven't already guessed, there's much more to a flawless wedding day than meets the eye. The more seamless it appears; the more effort has gone into planning and the more attention your service providers are paying to details as the day unfolds. It's just not possible to manage logistics on your big day and fully appreciate the magic and wonder of your wedding.

Are you ready to let go?

Allowing someone else to take charge may come easily for some. For others, like those who prefer to be in control or tend to be consumed by perfectionist tendencies, leaving management details to someone else will be difficult. However, if you spend the day trying to juggle every aspect of your wedding or worrying about achieving perfection, you'll miss the bliss. To you I say, let it go! Concentrate on the beautiful moment at hand. Relish every second of the ceremony and celebration and be fully present for the man of your dreams.

After organizing a thousand weddings over the years, I know the mere thought of relinquishing control creates high anxiety or even panic for some brides. About ninety-nine percent of my clients are super-duper organized. You know the type; they carry binders with color-coded tabs and alphabetize vendor contacts. They create spread sheets of their entire bridal party with everything from phone numbers and addresses to shoe sizes.

These organized clients are most often the ones who hire me.

It's my job to be the eyes, ears, hands, and feet for that organized bride. I become the person who ensures all her carefully devised plans come to fruition. During our consultations I ask detailed questions about every aspect of the day, right down to how the guest book table should be set up. Some brides stage their tables ahead of time and send me photos with such precise detail that I know how many inches to place the pen from the book and at what angle. I welcome this kind of input because I never have to guess what is wanted. My job is to make sure everything unfolds exactly as the bride has dreamed.

It's an honor to be able to create someone's dreams and to know the memories of those dreams will last a lifetime.

So, I ask once more: who is going to do all this for you on your wedding day?

If you think your aunt or cousin can manage to meet your exact specifications, think again. People are often surprised by this comment. It's not because your relatives don't care. They simply aren't professionals who know the ins and outs of wedding planning. They're not accustomed to bringing other people's dreams to life. Plus, there's a funny thing about family members. They often think their way is best. They believe they're doing the right thing by managing the details of your wedding to their own desires rather than to your specifications.

Can you imagine how devastating that would be for you, or how much trouble it could cause within your family?

When you get that ring, please for Pete's sake, book professional wedding assistance! Choose someone with great credentials and reviews. She or he will save you time, money, and frustration. A great planner will keep you sane during the process, deliver your day the way you ask for it, add more than a pinch of experience, and hopefully keep everyone laughing and having fun come rain or shine.

CHOOSING THE RIGHT SUPPORT

Wedding planners may appear to be the Jack or Jill of all trades, but not all wedding planners are created with the same skill sets. We all provide different services. Personally, the one thing I don't do is decorate. (I hear your collective gasp! That's right. I don't decorate.) I created my packages around my forte which is assisting the bride and her entourage. On the day of the wedding I help the bride and her bridesmaids get ready, and I keep them on schedule. There's no way I can drape chiffon on the walls while I'm steaming dresses, so I subcontract as necessary for other aspects of the wedding or have some of my team members step in, depending upon the budget.

Determine what your budget allows and how much support you need to pull off your special day. Ideally, you'll hire a full-fledged wedding planner, but if that isn't within your budget, you might consider hiring a wedding coordinator or a wedding designer, each of whom offers fewer but more specific assistance.

Let's take a closer look at each of these three professional services and what they provide.

► **The Wedding Planner:** A wedding planner can be hired up to two years before the wedding. Recently a bride contacted me to plan for a wedding date five years away. I had to be honest with her; I couldn't imagine discussing her wedding for five whole years. A lot could change in that time—her taste, her vision, and possibly even the groom! I invited her to reconnect when the wedding date is twenty-four months away.

A wedding planner contributes roughly thirty to one hundred hours or more to the planning process. A great planner can help you accomplish several tasks:

► Create your budget.

► Keep you within your budget.

► Create your timelines and floorplans.

► Provide a list of reputable vendors.

► Consider planning details that you might not even be aware of.

► Provide reliable advice and contacts that you don't have time to find on your own.

► Manage your wedding day so that you don't have to.

A wedding planner should be able to refer qualified vendors appropriate for your needs and budget and set up all vendor meetings. The planner should attend site tours and menu tastings with the you, walking through each venue to create layouts for optimum flow during the event.

In my full wedding planning package, I help the bride choose invitations. I proofread the invitation, address each one with handwritten calligraphy, and then stuff, seal, stamp the envelopes and mail them. All my packages include steaming or pressing the wedding gown and veil on site.

A wedding planner should attend the rehearsal and if needed, direct it as well. He or she should be present for the entire wedding day to troubleshoot, manage vendors, and coordinate the ceremony and reception.

A wedding planner isn't a wedding guest and should not behave like one by sipping champagne or visiting. My team and I barely get to eat let alone relax and enjoy the wedding. We continuously move from one stage of the event to the next. At the end of the evening, we clean things up and pack the bridal couple's items. Our role, after all, is to take all the stress and workload off the bride, the groom, and their parents.

At the end of the long emotional day, parents are always exhausted. In my full package, my staff and I pack up flowers, decorations, and other items when the evening is over, and we deliver them to a designated location. It's so rewarding to tell the bride's parents that everything is packed up. The look of appreciation in their eyes is worth everything to me!

If you don't have the time or knowledge to plan your own wedding, or you live out of state and could use the support of someone who is familiar with the area where you're getting married, a wedding planner can help. He or she will manage the ins and outs of your special day and every moment leading up to it. That allows you to enjoy your celebration to the fullest.

If you have the budget for a wedding planner, hire one.

► **The Wedding Coordinator:** If you don't have the budget for a full-fledged wedding planner or if you're determined to do most of the initial planning yourself, consider hiring a wedding coordinator. A wedding coordinator is focused on making sure your day unfolds as you want it to. He or she works on a much shorter timeline than a wedding planner and offers fewer services. Typically, a coordinator can be contracted between four weeks and twelve months before the wedding.

Coordinator duties are more limited than those of a wedding planner, so be sure to study the details of offered services before signing a contract. A good wedding coordinator will usually provide twenty to twenty-five hours of service managing various aspects of your wedding:

► Create an itinerary for the day.

► Confirm vendor attendance on the week of the wedding (although the vendors will have been previously booked by the bride).

► Attend the rehearsal.

► Attend the wedding ceremony and reception.

Hire a wedding coordinator if you decide to put in most of the advanced planning leg work. But it's important to ensure your plans keep you and your mother free from any tasks or chores on your wedding day. Your only focus should be looking your best, getting dressed, and saying "I do."

► **The Wedding Designer and Decorator:** The wedding designer and decorator's role is specifically aesthetic. He or she will create the wedding ambiance by consulting with you to create your vision within your budget. A designer can contribute sixty hours or more to your wedding. Their services are particularly beneficial if you need to dramatically recreate your venue space, for instance, in the case of a warehouse or a tent. A skilled designer can turn an empty shell into a magnificent ballroom. One of the best Wedding Designers I know is celebrity wedding planner and designer, David Tutera.

The wedding designer and decorator should provide support in several areas:

► Attend site visits and walk throughs to understand the event flow.

► Work with every aspect of design, including rentals, linens, lighting, draping, florals, candles, props, and required equipment.

► Set up all design and support elements on the day of the wedding and break it down at the end.

You can hire a designer to provide all the above services or just a few, depending upon your budget.

As you can see, not all wedding planners are decorators. Not all wedding coordinators are wedding planners. Each service provider will offer specific packages, contracts, and duties that suit their skills and preferences, but they should fall roughly within the areas outlined above: planning your entire wedding and managing your wedding day, just managing your wedding day, or creating your wedding aesthetic.

Your service person should be there to assist you in every way possible. On a few occasions I planned weddings that included the bride or groom's dog as a canine ring bearer. I found myself taking the dog outside to use the bathroom. Was that in my contract? No. But I went above and beyond the contract to make sure those brides had nothing to worry about but getting married.

Some tasks may not fall in my wheelhouse. Sometimes I'm not able to tackle a job that needs doing because something else I'm contracted to do is more pressing at that moment. On those occasions I make quick executive decisions and delegate to my team members or approach other vendors for assistance. It's my job to know where to focus my attention. Over two decades of wedding planning has given me a sixth sense about what is going on elsewhere and what's going to happen next.

At a recent quarterly meeting, I told my team that it takes a special person to be a wedding planner. It's an adrenaline rush! It's like jumping off a cliff every weekend and hoping that your parachute opens. Yet somehow every wedding works out, and I land on my feet. I'm prepared. My brides and grooms get married and they have fun.

Mission accomplished.

Planning Tips

1. Determine how much input and support you want, how much you can afford, and then choose your professional wedding support accordingly.

2. Be aware of how your service providers charge. Wedding planners can charge a flat fee, bill by the package, or charge a percentage of the entire cost of the wedding.

3. Wedding Coordinators can charge a flat fee, by the hour, or by the package.

4. Wedding designer fees vary widely depending upon the bride's budget and the amount of time and labor required to achieve her vision.

Secret Confession

A DAY IN THE LIFE

Wedding planners are prepared to spend ten to twelve hours juggling duties and troubleshooting their events. That's a long time to be "on." It gets extra-complex if more than one wedding is taking place at the same time. Let me tell you about the longest day ever.

On Mother's Day weekend in 2015 I had two weddings booked in New Orleans. Nothing unusual. I left my house at 6:30 a.m. that day. An hour-and-a-half later, I arrived at the Royal Sonesta on Bourbon Street to greet the bride and steam dresses for Wedding Number One—and I parked with no issues. Hallelujah! (If you don't know the area, finding parking is almost a miracle!) As I finished steaming all the dresses for Wedding Number One my assistant arrived to take the reins.

I then proceeded to the Sheraton on Canal Street for Wedding Number Two preparations. That was around 10:00 a.m. Roughly two hours later, I headed to the Immaculate Conception Church on Baronne Street for Wedding Number One. With five of my assistants—who happened to include my daughter and her best friend—we assembled a makeshift bar outside the church. After the ceremony we would hand guests daiquiris and hankies from there for the second line parade to the reception at the Royal Sonesta.

For those of you who aren't familiar with the custom, a second line parade consists of a small brass band (main line) that leads the bridal couple and their guests (the second line) to the reception with drinks and waving hankies. (Yes, in New Orleans, you can walk the streets with alcohol—as long as you have a permit, a police escort, and serve the liquor in plastic cups.)

As we were setting up, I learned that the Rolls Royce bringing Bride Number One to the Immaculate Conception Church from the Royal Sonesta had broken down. With some scrambling I made alternative arrangements for her. When she and her party arrived at the church, the church facility coordinator took charge of the processional and service. While the wedding took place, my assistants and I continued filling daiquiri cups. Soon the second line band, Big Pappa C, arrived along with police escorts on motorcycles.

We were ready.

When the front doors of the Immaculate Conception Church flew open, the band burst into Mardi Gras music. Two of my assistants passed out hankies for guests to wave at passersby, while the other assistants passed out daiquiris. When the bride and groom appeared, we handed them the traditional second line parade feathered umbrellas—white for the bride, black for the groom. As planned, the band took the lead, whisking the bridal party and their guests off to the reception at the Royal Sonesta where one of my assistants awaited their arrival.

We broke down the makeshift bar and headed back to the Sheraton on Canal Street Bride to help dress the bride, bridesmaids, and bride's mother for Wedding Number Two. As we finished preparations, we waited for the arrival of Wedding Number Two's transportation to the Holy Name of Jesus church on St. Charles Avenue. The brigade consisted of two large buses, each seating around fifty-five guests; a trolley for the bridal party; a stretch limo for the family; and a Rolls Royce for the bride and her father—complete with a police escort.

The front desk told me there were fourteen wedding parties at the Sheraton that weekend. Fourteen! That meant the hotel was surrounded by bridal party transportation. Fortunately, we were prepared. With signs indicating the bridal couple's names, my assistants directed everyone to the appropriate vehicles. (They later told me that we were the only ones to do this, thus avoiding the mass confusion experience by the other wedding parties. Kudos to us!)

When our police escort arrived and everyone was aboard the appropriate transportation, off they went. A text from my assistant let me know the reception for Wedding Number One at the Royal Sonesta was going well. I breathed a sigh of relief. By that time, it was 6:30 p.m. and I'd been going for twelve hours straight.

Little did I know I had eight hours more to go!

It was time to head to Pat O's on the River for Wedding Number Two's reception. Unfortunately, second line parades from hundreds of weddings across the city blocked roads everywhere. It took me almost five times as long as it should have to get there. Ugh! When I finally arrived, I quickly confirmed the setup for all of the bride's items such as the guest book table, favor table, pictures, and cake table. Then I went outside to greet the bridal party, who arrived before I did thanks to their police escort. (Brides, if you are having your wedding in New Orleans, you MUST get a police escort.)

Throughout the reception, my assistants and I hustled to meet every need of the bridal couple and their guests. At midnight, a horse and carriage arrived to whisk the bride and groom away. I cued the band to let guests know the evening was winding down. It took a while to get three hundred tipsy people down the venue escalator and out of the building to bid the bride and groom farewell, but we did it! Finally, the happy couple rolled away.

The day was done for them, but not for us. We began to gather up wedding gifts, leftover cake, the bride's items, and so on. At about 1:00 a.m., a bridesmaid returned to the ballroom looking for her cell phone. She was quite upset. We spent the next hour-and-a-half searching for it, and THEN we learned that a friend had picked it up for her earlier! It was now 2:30 a.m.—twenty hours since my day began.

Although I cannot begin to describe how tired I was, I was also elated by the experience of helping two couples celebrate their special day. I walked slowly back to my hotel room for a celebratory ice-cold beer, sat down, and put my aching feet up. I fell asleep in the chair. The next day was Mother's Day. My daughter took me out to a casual dinner to celebrate. I enjoyed it, but I was so stiff from my efforts the day before that I could barely move!

That kind of schedule is not uncommon in the wedding industry. I've had many similar weekends. As Donna Summer sang back in the 70s, "She works hard for the money."

I do—but what a wonderful way to earn a living!

FIRST THINGS FIRST

Creating a memorable day to celebrate the love of your life is what your wedding is all about. That takes great planning, and great planning requires a whole lot more than picking a venue or selecting your dress. It's about getting started with all the foundational elements in place. That includes a budget, incorporating traditions that are important to you into your celebration, and preparing yourself for circumstances that can arise as you, your friends, and family get caught up in the emotional whirlwind of wedding fever. So, let's put first things first.

THE WEDDING BUDGET

I cannot emphasize this enough: you need a budget, and you need it right away!

Establishing a wedding budge can be a challenge. Many brides I work with aren't sure exactly how much money they want to spend on their wedding, and they may have no idea how much weddings can cost. Costs vary according to the selected venue, of course, but they also depend upon the geographical location of your wedding. For example, in 2017 the average wedding in Baton Rouge cost just under half an average yearly salary. However, seventy miles down the road in New Orleans, the price could be nearly double or more. New York, Los Angeles, and Miami are exponentially higher.

You get the picture.

I strongly suggest that early in your engagement, you sit down with both sets of parents to discuss if they are willing and able to help pay for your wedding, and if so, how much they will contribute. It's particularly important to do this before the planning process begins. That way, you'll know exactly how much money you have to work with.

Long gone are the days when who paid for what was crystal clear. These days, the average age of brides and grooms has risen. They tend to be more established in their careers and are generally able to pay for at least part of their wedding. That gives them more control over the details. Years ago, when the bride's parents paid for everything, I often heard brides say, "Well, who's wedding is this?" when decisions were on the table. Her mother or father would typically respond, "And who's paying for this wedding?"

Any arguments that might arise can be eliminated by knowing from the start how many dollars the groom's parents, the bride's parents, and the bridal couple will contribute. If both sets of parents are remarried and there are more people to deal with, it's even more important to have the discussion about finances as soon as you get the ring on your finger.

If you're working on a tight budget, I offer a word of caution. Look at more than price when choosing vendors. You've probably heard the old cliché, "you get what you pay for." It's true. So, consider what aspect of your wedding day is the most important to you. Some brides point to the wedding gown, some are focused on photographs, while others are more concerned about the food or even the band. A bride once told me that the most important consideration for her wedding day was to serve top-shelf alcohol. Because she was on a tight budget, she chose an affordable wedding gown, hired a DJ rather than a live band, and saved money wherever else she could. It was a great reception! How could it not be when guests had drink selections like Grey Goose and Crown Royal to sip on? The key is to splurge on the details that are most important to you and cut back on things you deem less important.

Budget really matters, and if you don't keep careful tabs on where the money is going, expenses can go haywire. One bride's father offered to pay for the entire wedding—until he realized how much weddings cost. The bride had already begun contracting her dream venue and vendors. About two months before the wedding, her father called me to complain about costs. He was furious that his ex-wife, who was the mother of the bride, and the groom's parents were contributing little. I respectfully told him that the discussion about finances should have happened the second the couple got engaged. In the end, I dramatically reconfigured the bride's budget by changing the menu and scaling down flowers and decorations. Instead of an $80,000 wedding, she had a $40,000 wedding.

Even then, the situation grew scary when the vendor's balances were due. The bride's father was not paying them according to the contracts he had signed, and the vendors threatened to withhold services. Talk about stressful! Eventually, we worked things out. The wedding turned out beautifully. On the wedding day, the father of the bride told me I was his best friend and the best wedding planner ever! Whew!

Brides, please do yourself and your wedding planner a huge favor. Sit down with your parents and the groom's parents to discuss budgeting as soon as you are engaged.

SETTING THE DATE

One of the first things you'll do after you accept your groom's proposal—or he accepts yours—is set a date. If you have a specific wedding planner in mind, you may want to consult with her or him first for availability. On the other hand, if a certain date is important to you, you may want to set that first. Regardless, make sure you leave at least twelve months between your engagement and your wedding. That will give you more options for all aspects of your big day.

Think about it. If you only have three months to plan a wedding, your preferred venues, photographers, bands, videographers, florists, and caterers may already be booked. Even your choice of wedding gown could be impacted because many gowns are only available by special order. If you don't have much time, you may have to choose something off-the-rack instead of wearing your dream gown.

Leaving enough time will also give you some breathing room as you prepare, and it will ensure that any guests you really care about will have time to arrange their attendance.

THE VENUE SETS THE THEME

After you set your budget and hire your wedding planner, the next most logical step is to find your venue. Why, you may ask? Because the venue will establish the theme or set the stage for your wedding day, and that will impact all the decisions that follow.

Although your wedding planner should be able to provide you with some great suggestions for venues, ultimately, the choice is yours. Picture your wedding ceremony and reception in a variety of different settings. Consider the feeling or vibe you get when you imagine each one. For example, imagine a ceremony at a cathedral followed by a reception in a historical setting. Compare that to a garden ceremony and a reception in someone's beautiful home. Which ideas most resonate with you? Go for the vibe that suits you best!

Your venue selection will impact numerous other decisions like the décor you choose and the all-important dress. You would likely choose a different wedding gown for a church ceremony than you would choose for a beach-side ceremony.

Your aesthetic choices should be influenced by your venue. Whatever you choose will also impact your photographic memories of the day. One bride I worked held her reception in a gorgeous, elegant venue resembling a castle. Despite my advice for caution, she insisted on incorporating rustic-look décor. She chose burlap and mason jars as her motif. The homey, country feel of her décor contrasted sharply with the elegant backdrop of ornate stained-glass windows and stood out glaringly in every photo.

The venue you choose will reflect the type of reception you are planning and the traditions in your area of the country. Choosing a venue in South Louisiana is quite different than choosing a venue in the rest of the nation, for example. Down south, receptions usually last about three hours and food is typically served buffet style.

A big advantage of buffet style weddings is that you don't have to provide seating for everyone. Etiquette says that for buffet receptions it's acceptable to provide seating for approximately one third of your guests. In my experience, most brides are nervous about this and usually provide seating for half of their guests. There are always free seats available.

Receptions farther north are quite different. A five to six-hour celebration is typical with a cocktail hour followed by a full sit-down dinner with dancing. I grew up in North East Pennsylvania in a small coal mining town where wedding celebrations seemed to last the entire day. Ceremonies usually took place in the early afternoon around 2:00 p.m. followed by a bridal party picture session. The bridal party, family, and guests would meet at the reception venue around 5:00 p.m. for cocktails and hors d'oeuvres. A full sit-down dinner began around 6:00 p.m. followed immediately with dancing until midnight.

Determining the kind of reception you wish to have will help narrow down venue selection. Here in Baton Rouge we have a few Historical Venues that I call "empty shells." Brides bring their own furniture, décor, catering, bar, and flowers to transform these empty buildings into the venue of their dreams. Then there are some turnkey venues that offer everything from a facility coordinator to the linens and everything else, including the wedding cake. Your final choice will boil down to venue availability, your budget, and your style. The only limitation is your imagination.

On a side note, if you are not having a full sit-down dinner with seating for everyone, you do not need full place settings at the tables. This leads to a pet peeve of mine. Some brides love the appearance of colored chargers, linen napkins, and glassware at each seat, but think about it for a moment: if everyone isn't going to be seated, do only the "special" guests get the place setting? This does not fly with me. Do not do this! I've seen guests take their chargers up to the buffet line and use them as oversized dinner plates. Oh my gosh, how ridiculous! Please don't provide full place settings at your wedding unless you intend to provide a full sit-down dinner. It's best to keep it simple.

During the pre-planning stages, brides often choose vendors their friends have used. That's a great idea! After experiencing your friends' weddings, you'll know exactly what products and services you can expect to receive. If your friends were pleased with their results, chances are you will be too. There's nothing wrong with following their lead. Anything you can do to reduce risk and uncertainty or unknowns for your wedding day is always a great idea.

Figure out where your ceremony and reception will be. Choose your vendors. Then start searching for just the right wedding gown, the one that's perfect for the setting you've chosen and fits like a dream. (See Chapter 4 for detailed information about gown shopping.) Then everything else will fall into place. Choices become easier when you have a clear theme to follow.

BOOK YOUR REHEARSAL

Make sure to book your rehearsal as soon as possible. It is perhaps the single most important factor concerning the logistics of your ceremony. Why? Because the rehearsal makes sure every participant knows exactly where your ceremony will take place. Can you imagine the best man getting lost on the day of your wedding? What if you had to start without him?

You get the picture.

The rehearsal also provides the bridal party and participants with other important information, like exactly where to park, which entrance to use, where to report once they arrive, and a review of all other important information for your big day. If you don't rehearse, you'll have a frantic group of people on your hands for your wedding day!

Typically, rehearsals are scheduled for the night before the wedding, but in some cases, they might take place two nights before. Everyone involved will learn exactly where they should stand or sit for the ceremony. The bridal party will discover who is walking with whom and in what order. They can practice walking until they have the established the right pace. If immediate family members have not previously met, the rehearsal gives them a chance to get to know each other.

Usually, couples sign the marriage license at the rehearsal because it gives them one less thing to worry about on their wedding day. That reduces stress, and it takes about twenty minutes off the wedding day schedule. Please check with your officiant first. Not all of them are on board with this approach. If they are, I encourage you to take it.

People tend to run late, so I advise my brides to plan for it. If the rehearsal starts at six o'clock, tell everyone it starts at five-thirty to make room for latecomers and still be on time. A rehearsal should not last more than one hour. Over-rehearsing can cause confusion. Ending it in a timely manner shows respect for the venue and ensures you arrive at the rehearsal dinner on time.

Some churches have a facility coordinator who will open the church for your rehearsal and again on the wedding day. Make sure you or your wedding coordinator to have the facility coordinator's cell number, just in case.

When it's time for the rehearsal to begin, the officiant or priest will greet everyone. They may say a prayer. At that point, your wedding coordinator or planner will offer another greeting and some general announcements such as where the restrooms are or where to find the nursery for anyone with babies or small children. Then he or she will line everyone up.

I like to begin at the end to make sure everyone knows exactly where they're headed. I line everyone up at the altar area and direct family members to their seats. Once everyone is in place, I invite the officiant to share the last words he or she will speak at the ceremony. Usually, it's something to the effect of, "Ladies and gentlemen, may I present to you, Mr. and Mrs. Smith."

The couple will face their guests and recess, followed by the maid of honor with the best man and the rest of the bridal party. The bride's parents exit behind the bridal party, followed by the groom's parents.

When any of the bridal couple's grandparents are present, I encourage them to stay seated during the rehearsal and after the actual ceremony when the bridal party usually returns to the altar for pictures. Why make Grandma and Grandpa walk away and then stand around waiting?

After the recessional is reviewed, we begin practicing the entry. If the grandparents choose to rehearse their entry—which doesn't often happen—we begin with them. Usually, we start with the parents. The ushers will lead the groom's parents to their seats, then the bride's. The bridal party rehearses their entry, followed by the bride and her father. When they reach the altar area, the groom steps forward to meet them.

At the altar, the officiant will run through ceremony basics. The planner will offer a few tips about how the bridal party should stand, what to do with the bride's flowers and the rings, and who should move where, when. I always remind others to watch out for the bride's train. I've seen too many fathers so consumed with emotion that they've tripped over it!

If you have readers or speakers other than the officiant, it's helpful to let them stand in position and practice a few lines through the microphone. If the marriage license isn't being signed at the rehearsal, the couple can rehearse how the signing will unfold on the wedding day.

After the ceremony run-through and another rehearsal of the recessional, the bridal couple can sign the marriage license if they've chosen to do it ahead of time.

As I mentioned earlier, the entire rehearsal should only take an hour at most. Then you can move on to your rehearsal dinner and relax.

WEATHER

Weather is a concern for most brides regardless of where or when they're planning to get married. If you live in Louisiana like me, especially South Louisiana, the chance of rain on your big day is probably fifty percent no matter what time of year you marry. Summer is our official rainy season, and top of that—just for added interest—hurricane season starts then too.

Once June first hits, you can be sure rain will fall every day around four o'clock in the afternoon until about five. It's usually steam-room steamy right after. Things improve slightly in the fall, but even then, our weather can be unpredictable. Hurricanes have struck as late as November. Winters are wet as well.

In South Louisiana, March, April, and May are the best months for weddings. That's when my team, all our vendors, and other planners across the region are busiest. During some spring seasons, I've had thirty plus weddings on the go! Regardless of the time and location, if an outside ceremony or reception is involved, I always create a Plan B in case of bad weather. Make sure you do too. I'm happy to say that of the one thousand weddings I have planned and coordinated, only a few have been rained on. I like to think I'm a good luck charm!

WEATHERING RELATIONSHIPS

Other kinds of storm clouds have the potential to gather as you plan for your wedding. Emotions can run high and that means tension can rise too. Sometimes the stress of the situation makes people you love and care about act in surprising ways. If you're aware of such possibilities right from the start, you won't be caught off guard.

> ► **Reticent Grooms:** The man of your dreams might be ready to get married, but that doesn't mean he's into planning the big event. Grooms usually aren't wedding experts. They haven't dreamed about fantasy weddings since childhood like many girls do, and sometimes their efforts to get involved or the suggestions they make are rejected.

I once watched a groom try to help his bride choose the wedding invitations. When he pointed out the invitation he liked, the bride criticized his choice using humiliating words like "stupid" and "ugly." When the groom remained silent throughout the rest of the planning process, she wondered why.

So, brides, try and be understanding. Most grooms are only comfortable making decisions about details they really understand. You know your groom. Delegate tasks to him that he would find interesting. Perhaps that might be planning the honeymoon or choosing music for the reception. Guys usually enjoy testing out menus and cake so make sure he is included for all tastings. And give him a break when he isn't comfortable making the decisions at hand.

> **Jealous Bridesmaids:** Yes, jealous bridesmaids are a thing and almost every bride has to deal with at least one. Sometimes a jealous bridesmaid has even been a friend of the bride for years. She agreed to be in the wedding out of feelings of obligation rather than a sense of joy and support for the bride. She may be jealous of all the attention the bride is getting or she may feel helpless and resentful about decisions the bride makes that impacts her pocketbook—like the bride's selection of bridesmaid dresses, for example. Or she could be envious of the groom and the fact that her friend found a wonderful man to marry. The reasons are endless. So are the possibilities for trouble.

A bridesmaid seething with jealousy can create all kinds of misery. She might not participate in all the functions prior to the wedding. She could drag her feet when it comes time to order her bridesmaid dress. She might even try to sabotage celebrations like the bachelorette party or attempt to turn other bridesmaids against the bride.

How do you deal with this?

Carefully.

I'm not a psychologist, but I have noticed that communication is key. Should you encounter a problem with one of your bridesmaids, be willing to speak about it with her gently and lovingly, in private.

> **Disgruntled Relatives:** The stressful high emotional state of weddings tends to highlight or even aggravate any existing challenges in family relationships. All families

have some level of disfunction hiding somewhere in the closet. Old memories or hurts rise to the surface. Differences in opinion become prickly, especially in the new but fragile relationships between families of the bride and groom. Whether it's the groom's sister, the bride's stepmom, or a great aunt, there is almost always at least one relative whose behavior wreaks emotional havoc or worse. Sometimes it's even parents of the bride or groom.

People's feelings are easily hurt too. In one wedding, the sister of the groom had ruffled feathers when she wasn't invited to be a bridesmaid, even though she and the bride weren't close. I always remind my brides and grooms that they can't please everyone. Someone is sure to be disappointed with the decisions they make, but it's their wedding. Be kind to everyone but try not to let their unhappiness spoil yours.

Weddings really do bring out the best and worst in people. You might want to consider who among your friends and family could potentially create problems for you and how you might respond to them if it happens.

WEDDING TRADITIONS TRIED, TRUE, QUIRKY, AND NEW

As you dream about your wedding, consider any traditions that are important to you and include them in your plans from the start.

You've probably heard the old English rhyme, "Something old, something new, something borrowed, something blue, and a sixpence in your shoe." It launched the most common traditions about what to wear on the day of your wedding to ensure good luck. Let's take a closer look at what each of those items represents and how you can incorporate them into your wedding.

▶ **Something Old:** "Something old" brings a symbol of continuity into your marriage ceremony. It could be a token belonging to the bride's grandmother or one representing a family tradition or a special memory.

▶ **Something New:** Your wedding gown, your veil, your headpiece, perfume—anything that is new to you— represents optimism for your future. It's probably one of the easiest items to include.

▶ **Something Borrowed:** Anything you borrow from a loved one that has strong sentimental value for the person who lends it to you symbolizes happiness. Whether it's a hankie, a piece of jewelry, or even a veil, knowing you are well-connected and surrounded by love brings joy to your big day.

▶ **Something Blue:** Whether it's the ribbon on your garter, the lace on your hankie, or even the color of your bra or panties, blue packs a lot of symbolism. It represents purity, loyalty, love, and fidelity. Use your imagination to select "something blue," and have fun with it!

▶ **Sixpence in Your Shoe:** A sixpence is an old British coin that hasn't been used for decades, but it's a symbol of good luck and prosperity. Because these coins are hard to get hold of, it's fine to place a penny in your shoe for good luck.

These are all sweet traditions with beautiful meanings, especially when the tokens used to represent them come from loved ones. Make sure your photographer captures a picture of your "something old, something new, something borrowed blue" and your sixpence or penny to represent the special story of how you accumulated them.

You may wish to let other commonly held traditions play a role on your wedding day too, and you may be curious about where they come from.

► **Wedding Rings:** The circular form of engagement and wedding rings is a symbol of eternal love and faithfulness. They are worn on the fourth finger of the left hand because Ancient Romans believed a vein in that finger ran directly to the heart.

► **White Wedding Dresses:** Thank Queen Victoria for this one! Before her marriage to Prince Albert of Saxe-Coburg and Gotha in 1840, wedding gowns as we now know them didn't exist. A bride would either buy a stylish new dress or wear the best one she had.

► **Wedding Veils:** Although the wedding veil has different meanings for different cultures and faiths, it is generally agreed that it originated in ancient Rome. Brides wore the veil to ward off any evil spirits that might try to spoil her happiness.

► **Giving the Bride Away:** In days gone by, marriages were contractual arrangements. Women and their possessions were considered the property of their fathers until they married. When a father gave his daughter away to a groom, it signified relinquishing her care and property into the hands of her new husband. These days when a bride walks down the aisle toward her groom, she goes with her father as a sign of honor and respect. The question, "Who gives this woman to be married?" still arises during wedding ceremonies but it's more custom than legality, and usually both of the bride's parents respond.

► **No Peeking!** You've probably heard the old superstition that it's bad luck for the bride and groom to see each other before the ceremony on their wedding day. When you know the history of this superstition it makes sense. Sort of. In the old days when arranged marriages were common, an engaged couple might not even be allowed to MEET before their wedding. The reason? The groom might take one look at his bride and call off the wedding! While some couples still abide by this practice as tradition rather than superstition, more and more couples are having a "first look," an opportunity to see each other and have a few photos taken prior to the ceremony.

► **The Bouquet Toss:** Brides have carried bouquets since ancient times as a symbol of good luck, faithfulness, and fertility, but throwing it came about as a form of rescue. Hundreds of years ago, it was considered good luck to touch the bride or leave the wedding celebration with a piece of her attire. People would crowd around trying to touch her or rip away a piece of her dress. Eventually, in an attempt to distract guests, she would throw her bouquet instead and make a break for it with her new husband. Today, bouquets are tossed to the bridesmaids or single women attending a wedding. Superstition says that whoever catches the bouquet will be the next to catch a husband.

► **The Garter Toss:** Apparently garter tossing evolved from the same touch-the-bride-for-good-luck tradition that spurred the bouquet toss. Instead of allowing guests to ravage his new wife's dress, the groom tossed the bride's garter for good luck. These days, the bride sits on a chair or the best man's lap and the groom slides off her garter. He tosses it into a crowd of all the single men at the wedding. The man to catch it is the next man to be married. We all know that guys are usually more reluctant to get married than women are so that might explain why guys are often hesitant to line up for the garter toss.

► **The Money Dance:** Years ago, newlyweds greeted each guest as they exited the church following their wedding ceremony. That rarely happens anymore. Think of the money dance as a lucrative receiving line where each guest has the opportunity to greet the newlyweds and dance around the room with the bride or groom. In return, they pin money to the groom's clothing or place it in the bride's purse or a basket held by one of her bridesmaids. The tradition is said to have originated in Poland. It seems to be one that people either love or hate.

► **Throwing Rice or Confetti:** The tradition of throwing rice at the bridal couple is another gift from Ancient Rome. Showering couples with rice celebrated fertility and the expansion of family wealth and resources. These days rice is considered a health hazard for birds and other wildlife, so it has been replaced with items like biodegradable confetti or flower petals.

► **Wedding Cake:** Today's beautiful wedding cakes emerged from a number of countries and traditions. They range from a wheat or barley cake used to bless the bride in Ancient Rome to a savory pie served to wedding guests in Europe. Eventually the elaborately decorated wedding cake emerged, and it came to represent the wealth and status of the bride's family.

Wedding cake has become a popular symbol of weddings, probably because of the wide array of traditions that have evolved around it. Here are a few of them:

► *White Wedding Cake.* White icing symbolized money in Victorian times, and wedding cakes were a symbol of celebration and wealth used to represent the bride.

► *Cake cutting.* In years gone by the bride would typically cut the cake by herself to signify the loss of her virginity. Now the bride and groom cut it together. His hand under hers symbolizes support—and it makes a great photo op!

► *Bride and groom feeding each other wedding cake.* This activity symbolizes the bridal couple's commitment to take care of each other. Like cake-cutting, it makes another terrific—if sometimes messy—photo op!

► *Saving the top tier of the wedding cake.* Many couples save the top layer of a wedding cake and put it in their freezer, carefully wrapped, to share on their first anniversary or upon the christening of their first child.

► *Wedding Cake Pulls.* The tradition of tucking silver or gold charms under the wedding cake has its roots in the U.K. and is popular in the New Orleans area today. Each charm has a long ribbon attached that drapes out from under the cake. Bridesmaids or the bride's single friends are invited to gather around the cake, take a ribbon, and pull out a charm. Each charm has a special meaning. For example, pulling a ring means the recipient will be the next to marry. An airplane or boat represents a trip, while a four-leaf clover signifies good luck.

► *Sleeping with a slice of wedding cake under your pillow.* Folklore dating back some three hundred years suggests single female wedding guests who tuck a piece of wedding cake under their pillow and sleep on it will dream about their future husband. If the cake isn't well wrapped, it could turn out to be a crumby sleep!

Here are a few other quirky traditions I've recently come across. Maybe some of them will resonate with you.

► **Marry on the Upswing:** According to an old Chinese custom, getting married when the minute hand of the clock is moving upwards will bring the couple special blessings. Instead of scheduling the ceremony for six o'clock in the evening, this tradition suggests that it's luckier to hold it at half past the hour.

► **Burying the Bourbon:** An old Southern tradition I recently learned about says that burying a bottle of bourbon one month before the wedding at the site of the ceremony will ensure there's no rain on the day of the wedding. The bottle must be full and buried upside down, and it should be buried on a day of good weather—the kind you'd like for the wedding.

63

The night before the wedding, rain or shine, the bottle of bourbon should be dug up and shared with the entire wedding party to guard against bad weather. In some cases, the bottle is dug up after the ceremony and shared at the wedding. Either way, bourbon drinking will happen. This fun, crazy tradition is one that I will share with my future brides!

> ► **Drops of Rain:** Even with the best possible planning—buried bourbon aside—there are no guarantees about the weather. Some cultures say that a rainy wedding day symbolizes purity and fertility, but no matter how you look at it, if the weather goes awry be prepared to make the best of things.

One lovely tradition does just that. It can take the damper out of a rainy wedding day in the nicest possible way. Simply gather some of the rain and use it to baptize your first born. How beautiful is that?

I shared the idea with one of my June brides while she was getting her hair and makeup done. The weather was looking good and the chance of rain was only ten percent which is odd for a June wedding in Louisiana. Once we arrived at the church and got settled, I checked the front doors to make sure they were unlocked for the guests. To my surprise, it was raining and raining hard. Time to put that tradition to work.

I frantically searched for a container to collect some rain. All I could find was the tin box holding the programs. I removed the programs and placed the box outside. The rain only lasted about two minutes, but I gathered enough to pour in a small zip baggy. I labeled it "Rain drops on your wedding day for your first baby's baptism."

Since then, I carry a small container to gather rain, should it happen to fall, and a special bottle to place it in as the lovely keepsake.

Planning Tips

1. Make sure you set a wedding date that allows enough time to book the venues and vendors you want. Allow enough time to order the perfect wedding gown.

2. Establish a budget IMMEADIATELY and determine who will pay for what.

3. Select your venue before making any other plans.

4. If your plans include any outdoor activities, make sure Plan B is ready to go in case of inclement weather.

5. Be ready to encounter relationship complications as you prepare for your wedding. They happen.

6. As you plan, incorporate any traditions that are important to you.

Secret Confession

DEAR FATHERS

The incredible movie, Father of the Bride, is one of my all-time favorites. Starring Steve Martin as George Banks, this beautiful, feel-good movie taps into a father's deep thoughts and emotions about his daughter's wedding—and a whole lot of talk about money. The eccentric, expensive wedding planner, "Franck," played by Martin Short, sparks questions from George about why, exactly, a wedding coordinator is required. That's something I often encounter with real-life dads too.

I suspect the whole charade about money is about something else altogether. In the movie, George is upset that his daughter, his little girl, is about to get married. Being angry about the cost of her wedding is a great cover for his feelings about "losing" his daughter, who like all children grew up too fast. Weddings have a way of bringing out all kinds of feelings, don't they?

Dads tend to focus on the bottom line. When I meet prospective brides and their moms, many of them say, "Well, we'll have to talk to Dad and see if we can get his approval to hire you." That's when I wish I could talk to the dads personally. Some of my biggest skeptics are fathers who later become my biggest fans.

I met with one of my brides and her mom in her mom's kitchen while her dad sat in the living room reading the paper. He shouted from his chair, "Allie, you're not going to spend all my money, are you?"

I laughed and replied, "No sir! As a matter of fact, I'm going to save you money!" He grunted and whispered, "Yeah, right."

I really had to prove myself to this family and especially the dad. I did it! After the wedding, the bride's parents quickly spread the word about how much I helped them, and voila! I had a lot of business coming my way from their friends' daughters—at least ten more weddings! I am very grateful for that.

The skeptical dad praised my services so much that when his second daughter got engaged, he said, "Call Allie!" What a testimony to what I do. Once dads realize that my services are more than just window dressing, they're hooked.

Another father of the bride told me, "Allie, you were worth every penny. When I heard my wife and daughter complaining and stressing, all I had to do was say, 'Call Allie. She'll take care of it.' And they did call, and you did take care of everything."

Yet another dad, Henry, told me his favorite part of my service was at the reception when I kept handing him his favorite cocktail, Makers Mark and water, throughout the evening. He never had to wait in line in the bar.

Following the wedding of his first daughter, one father, Brent, told his other recently engaged daughter he had two requests. The first, she was to hire a certain band. The second? "You must hire Allie!"

Now that's a fan!

So, dads don't worry. I won't spend all your money. In fact, I will save you money in the long run by guiding your daughter in the planning process and helping her every step of the way. I will ensure no mistakes are made, that your vendors are reputable with top notch products and services, and I will be your go-to person when the you-know-what hits the fan at your house and it seems like your wife and daughter are losing their minds.

You too will say hiring a wedding planner was worth every penny.

WEDDING ATTIRE

Dressing up for weddings is a must! Although planning a wedding involves considering the attire of the bridal party and close relatives like parents and grandparents, one of the most exciting decisions concerns picking out your wedding gown. So, let's start there.

Lots of factors come into play when you go gown shopping, like your dreams, taste, budget, timeline, and even who you choose to go shopping with. One of the primary factors influencing your choice is the venue and the location of you wedding which is why you need to make those decisions first. The venue creates the atmosphere or setting for the day, and you'll want to choose a gown that is appropriate and comfortable in that setting, something that works for the climate and the season.

ORDER YOUR GOWN WITH MONTHS TO SPARE

Do you know the real reason why engagements are a year in length? Because sometimes it takes that long for the wedding gown to be delivered and to make all the alterations necessary for a perfect fit.

Brides occasionally luck out and find a dress on the rack that fits them like a glove, but not very often. Chances are you won't be one of those lucky few and you'll probably have to order your wedding gown to get the right fit. It can take anywhere from one month to seven for the dress to arrive. The wisdom is clear. Give yourself plenty of time when choosing your wedding gown.

But what if you want to get married right away? You can always find a gown in a pinch. You won't have as many options as the person who has a year to prepare, but it's doable if you're flexible and open minded about the dress. It's possible to purchase a dress off the rack, get alterations the same day, and walk out with the wedding gown steamed, pressed and ready to go. Though I have seen it happen in instances where couples want to elope, it's rare. The more time you have, the more choice you will have, and that will give you a greater opportunity to find the dress of your dreams to wear as you walk down the aisle.

Generally, wedding gown orders take up to seven months to arrive. Even just hemming the gown and making a couple of minor alterations could add on another two months. If you're a bride in the South where bridal portrait sessions are the norm, you'll need an additional six weeks to two months to accommodate a photo session for you in your wedding gown ahead of the big day. Suddenly, eleven months have flown by.

If you really want options—and truly, there are millions of them—give yourself at least twelve months for your engagement.

However, I don't recommend an engagement longer than a year unless you are paying for your own wedding and you need the time to save up money.

GOWN STYLES

With an endless array of styles to choose from, how do you begin to decide on the wedding gown that's perfect for you? Your personal taste plays a role, but it isn't the only factor.

When I worked at that bridal shop in Baton Rouge, I was always floored by the number of brides who came in shopping for their wedding gown even though they had nothing else planned, not even a wedding date! Some even came in without a ring, others without even a promise of a ring! It quickly became clear that the first thing most brides dream about is the wedding gown.

That just may be a bit backward, however. Let me explain why. What if you find the most beautiful heavy satin ball gown? A gown encrusted with the finest rhinestones and finished with a semi-cathedral length train. You fall in love with it. You purchase it. You are so happy you found "the one."

Then a little while later, you and your fiancé take a vacation at a beach resort. You witness a wedding ceremony taking place at sunset. The water is emerald green, the sands are sugar white. As the sun descends in a red gold glow, you both suddenly feel this is the perfect spot for your ceremony.

So, would you wear that heavy ball gown with the semi cathedral length train? You could wear it—anything is possible—but would you really want to? Or would you rather go barefoot and wear something simpler, say a light, breezy chiffon wedding dress?

That scenario illustrates why it is usually best to decide your date and venue before you purchase your wedding gown. The time of year your wedding takes place determines the weather, and that impacts your decision too. You wouldn't want to wear a long-sleeved velvet wedding gown in the summer. It would be hot and sticky and would look out of place against a summery background. Your wedding photographs will be a forever reminder of your misstep.

Location matters too, as I've mentioned. Think of the most beautiful Cathedral Church with the longest aisle you have ever seen. An ornate altar with a huge pipe organ. Gold crown molding and marble pillars. This is the kind of church that takes your breath away when you enter and makes you immediately feel you must whisper reverently. Could you sport a sexy, short cocktail dress as a wedding gown in this venue? Probably not. On the other hand, a garden wedding would look lovely with a tea length, lace overlay dress with a full skirt.

If you happen to have a royal bloodline, that could affect your choice of wedding gowns too, although not many brides could pull off the dress Meghan Markle wore on her wedding day. (She actually wore two; one for the church ceremony itself and a slightly sexier, off the shoulder version for the reception.) Anyway, I think you see the point. The venue, climate, and time of year help to create a theme. Choosing your gown with a theme in mind will help your whole day feel more cohesive and a lot more comfortable.

WHOSE DECISION IS IT?

When I first entered the wedding business in 1996, I worked at a bridal shop. I saw some crazy things over the ten years I worked there. If reality shows had existed back then, we would have had the number one show on television!

Many brides brought along an entourage of friends and relatives who turned out to be negative naysayers; people who criticized each dress the bride tried on, stitch by stitch. It was certainly counterproductive. Sadly, brides still tend to bring along too many "helpers" today. Perhaps some people think they are being helpful by pointing out everything they don't like, but it destroys the bride's confidence and rules out some dresses that might be strong contenders, all because of personal taste.

So, in the dress-shopping department, my number one suggestion is for you to begin by looking at gowns on your own. If you simply can't muster up the courage to go alone or you just want to share the excitement of exploring, then I advise you to take along one friend or your mom. But no more than one other person whom you deeply trust.

Don't forget to wear a proper bra and shapewear. Bring your shoes too. Those crucial items will help you view any dress you try on at its best.

For the most part, brides know their body type and what looks good on them. But here's the thing; wedding gowns have different considerations. For example, if you're short, you'll look even shorter in a ball gown. If you're voluptuous, a tightly fitted gown with flares will accentuate every curve of your body.

An experienced bridal consultant can take one look at you and have a fairly good idea what styles will flatter your size and shape so go into the bridal salon with an open mind. Give the consultant the latitude to show you a few dresses that you might not have otherwise considered. You may be surprised. I've seen it often— brides ending up with a dress they would have never noticed on the rail, let alone dreamed of trying on in the first place. Test all types of necklines and skirt types. Try on the most elaborate dress complete with all the bling and then slip on a simple silk wedding gown with no embellishments at all.

Which one lights you up?

When I worked at the bridal shop, I'd watch each bride respond to every dress she tried on. Sometimes she wouldn't leave the dressing room. At other times, she'd twist and turn to study every inch of the dress in the mirror, smiling all the while. That reaction made the dress a definite "maybe." But if she took one glimpse in the mirror and started crying, and the mother of the bride started crying, and the staff started crying, it was time to pull out the credit card. She had found her dress.

If you long to have your entire entourage of friends and relatives weighing in on the dress like they do on reality TV shows, you'll find it easier to survive their comments if you do some preliminary work. Pick out your top three dresses. Show those three and only those three to your entourage. Whatever they choose will be something you like.

BEWARE OF SIZE LABELS!

Warning! Warning! Wedding gowns are cut according to European sizes. Those sizes run smaller than they do in the U.S.—and not just by a little. If you are typically a size eight in the U.S., your wedding gown may be a ten or even a twelve.

Unfortunately, I've heard brides sob, "I have never worn a size ten in my life! I can't walk down the aisle in a size ten!" For whatever reason, we women often allow the size of our clothes to tank our feelings of self-worth. But please don't panic! You'll still wear your usual size in regular clothes. Nothing has changed but a number on one dress. Psych yourself up ahead of time knowing that in all likelihood, the size label sown inside your wedding gown will not match the label in your regular street clothes. You simply need to get over the size thing. You'll live, and you'll still look beautiful. Nothing has really changed.

Don't let the number put you off. Just find a stunning gown that fits you.

ALTERATIONS

Yay! You get the call from the bridal shop. Your wedding gown has arrived! You are excited and just can't wait to try it on—which is what I suggest you do as soon as you get the call. Why? You want to make sure the dress they are calling about is the right dress in the size and color you ordered.

So, try the dress on. However, if your wedding is still about six months away, I recommend waiting to have any alterations made. Twelve weeks before or your wedding day—or the date of your bridal portrait session if you're having one—is sufficient. As we all know, stress can cause weight gain or loss, and planning a wedding is stressful. All those showers, announcement parties, bachelorette parties, plus the stress of your regular job can impact how your wedding dress will fit. If you make alterations too soon and you lose or gain weight, you'll have to get it altered again.

One of my best friends, Jeanne, has been a seamstress for thirty years. She's now the alterations manager for a bridal shop. She tells me that brides gaining or losing weight is one of the most frustrating situations to deal with. She will tell the bride, "Stay at this exact weight! Don't gain or lose anymore. The dress fits you perfectly right now as it is!"

But nine times out of ten the bride returns for new alterations.

If you lose a considerable amount of weight, the dress may need such drastic alterations that it won't look like the same dress anymore. If you gain a considerable amount of weight, the seamstress can add gussets or fitted panels to the sides of the gown, but they are noticeable for sure. The worst-case scenario: you may need to buy a new gown.

My seamstress friend reminds me that brides need to wear proper underwear to their fitting, just as they did when they were trying on dresses. Some brides can get away without a bra and just sew cups into the dress. Others can't. It's best to invest in a great bra to give your bust the most flattering shape. Consider wearing some type of slimming shapewear if your dress happens to be a slinky sheath that reveals every nook and cranny of your body. Shapewear may not be the sexiest form of lingerie for your wedding night, but it beats having all your guests staring at your bulging thong during the ceremony.

It's important to note that gowns are not only sized smaller than what we're used to but designed for women who are five feet nine inches in height. The average woman is five inches shorter, so the chances are good your dress will need hemming. My seamstress friend tells me some brides try and forego the hem to save money. When that happens, she encourages them to attempt walking in the dress. They always end up tripping. Don't skim on the hem of your gown. Take your seamstress's advice.

Just as it's important to wear the proper undergarments to your fitting, it's important to wear your wedding shoes or another pair of shoes with the exact heel height to get the hem right. If your dress requires a slip, wear that too. The slip can alter the hemline of the gown.

DRESSES FOR BRIDESMAIDS AND MOTHERS

Some brides know exactly what they want their bridesmaids to wear and have no problem telling them so. This is the dress. Period. Not up for discussion. Other brides might choose the color and fabric and then let each bridesmaid pick their own style.

I love the latter idea because not all body types are alike. One style dress might look incredible on some and not so great on others. By allowing each bridesmaid to choose a style that fits and flatters her body type perfectly, your bridesmaids will feel more comfortable physically and psychologically for your wedding day. If your bridesmaids are more comfortable, you and they will be happier. In my opinion, it also adds some interest and variety to the photos. However, if you are a bride who would prefer everyone wears the same dress, that's okay too! Remember, it's your day. You call the shots.

Some brides have an exceedingly difficult time choosing the right dress and ask their bridesmaids for input. While that might seem like the logical thing to do, it invites the potential for a whole lot of trouble. Everyone will have opinions and complaints to offer. That can be overwhelming for the bride and possibly send her into a tailspin. Sometimes arguments ensue. I've even seen bridesmaids drop out because they do not like the dress or create such a fuss that the bride is forced to eliminate them from the wedding entirely. Yikes!

I have some advice for the undecided bride. Follow the same suggestion offered about choosing your wedding gown. Choose your favorite three dresses and let the bridesmaids vote. Problem solved.

Brides should be conscientious about pricing when selecting dresses for the attendants. Expenses mount quickly when a bridesmaid must purchase a dress, shoes, and jewelry, and pay for special hair and makeup for the wedding day—not to mention the costs associated with related parties and showers.

Steering clear of extreme fashions or fads when choosing bridesmaids' dresses is also a good idea. Stick with classic or simple styles. Remember the movie *27 Dresses*? Katherine Heigl's character, Jane Nichols, was a bridesmaid twenty-seven times and saved each dress, none of which she wore again. Some were hideous.

A bride should set a deadline for her bridesmaids to order their dresses, and that deadline should be no less than six months before the wedding. It may take three months for the dresses to come in and another month for alterations. That leaves a buffer zone in case any emergencies arise. What emergencies, you ask? Well, I've planned many weddings where a bridesmaid or even two become pregnant. Some girls go on drastic diets because they want to look super-hot for the wedding and they lose two dress sizes. With a healthy buffer zone, there's time to order another dress in a larger or smaller size if necessary, which may be more effective than altering the original dress drastically and changing the way it looks. I overheard one of my past brides tell her bridesmaids, "Do not get pregnant before my wedding or I will kill you!"

I cannot make this stuff up, folks.

So, let me repeat; brides must give their bridesmaids a deadline date to order their dresses. Some girls will drag their feet to order because they want to lose a few pesky pounds first. Other girls don't have the funds available and are embarrassed to tell the bride. But the bride must remain firm with her the deadline. She should communicate to them how long the dresses take to come in and the time frame required for alterations. There is no time to waste. If a bridesmaid does not order in time, the bride may have to give her another role in the wedding such as a greeter or a reader. This is where things get sticky. If such occasions arise, I always tell my brides to blame the deadline on me. This situation is rare, but it can happen. Please be prepared.

MOTHER'S DRESSES

Most moms wait until the last minute to order their dresses. They are so focused on their daughters and other tasks on their "to do" lists that they forget about themselves. As a mom, I can relate to this. However, moms should order their dresses six months before the wedding too so they can avoid risking disappointment with the "off the rack" scramble.

To ensure each the mother of the bride and the mother of the groom are distinguished and set apart, the mother of the bride should choose her dress color first. Of course, each mom should choose a color that coordinates with the bridal party.

CHOOSING THE RIGHT DRESS LENGTH

Dress style is important, but so is dress length. A certain hierarchy is at play here; the appropriate length for all dresses is determined by the length of the bridal gown, but the length of the mother of the groom's dress is determined by the length of the mother of the bride's dress. Sound confusing? It's really not that bad.

Whether the bridal gown is knee length, tea length (mid-calf), ballerina length (between mid-calf and ankle) or floor length, dresses for the bridesmaids, mothers, and grandmothers can either match its length or go shorter, but not longer. The mother of the groom's dress length should either match or be shorter than the mother of the bride's dress.

See? Easy peasy.

THE MOST IMPORTANT ACCESSORY: TUXEDOS!

No bridal gown or bridesmaid dress is complete without a tuxedo or suit by its side. In my experience, it's far easier to choose formal wear for the groom and his attendants than it is for a bride to choose her wedding gown or find dresses that her bridesmaids can all agree upon. Regardless of the tuxedo or suit chosen, the results are always stunning. As we all know, everyone is wild about sharply dressed men!

Tuxedos or suits are usually ordered around six to eight months before the wedding. The classic look of a black tuxedo with a bow tie is always in style, but lately brides are drawn to navy tuxedos or fitted navy suits. Light gray tuxedos or suits constructed of lightweight fabrics do well in the summer compared to the heavy wool found in black tuxedos.

If you've ever walked into a tuxedo shop, you'll know that all the pants and shirts look the same. In the end, styling comes down to your choice of jackets, ties, vests, and sometimes cummerbunds. In the past, the groom and groomsmen traditionally wore vests, cummerbunds, and a bow tie or necktie to match the bridesmaid's dresses. These days, it's more common to match ties and perhaps a pocket square tucked into the upper pocket on the left side of the jacket.

If you use pocket squares, make sure your groom and his attendants determine how to fold them before the wedding day. There are countless approaches to choose from. If the style of fold isn't determined ahead of time, you may end up with an array of options in your wedding photos—from square, flared, or feathered folds, or perhaps even bunched up and shoved into the pocket! Matching groomsmen offer a more refined presentation.

Brides frequently ask if the fathers, grandfathers, and ushers should match the groom and groomsmen by wearing the same tuxedo or suit. Grandfathers do not have to match unless they choose to. As dads are not technically in the wedding party, they may prefer to coordinate their outfits with the moms, who will likely wear colors that go well those of the bridal party. Ushers are considered members of the bridal party, but they aren't groomsmen. That puts them in a slightly different category. They may wear tuxes or a suit at the discretion of the bride and groom.

Another common question concerns which buttons should be buttoned on the tuxedo or suit. Button the lone button on a single-button jacket. In a two or three-button jacket, the bottom button is always left undone. Why? It goes way back to the early 1900s when King Edward VII always unbuttoned the last button of his waistcoat because he was too fat! (I'm not kidding. You can Google it. Crazy how we still honor traditions from way back when without knowing why.)

Just as brides must always try on their bridal gowns, the groom, groomsmen, ushers, and dads must try on their attire before they leave the store—the whole suit, complete with shirt and accessories. Typically, pickup takes place the day before the wedding. If the jacket is too tight, the sleeves of the shirt too long, or the pants too short, the tuxedo shop has time to make any adjustments. If pickup takes place on the day of the wedding, they can wait for the adjustments to be made on the spot. Whenever a guy shows up to the wedding with an ill-fitting tuxedo or suit, I know he did not try it on before he left the store.

Some tuxedo shops have adopted a policy requiring the customer to initial the receipt before leaving the store to acknowledge he tried everything on, and it fit well. Then it becomes his responsibility if it doesn't fit correctly. Bravo!

These days, many bridal parties come in from out of town for their friends' weddings. Rented tuxedos or suits usually need to be returned the day following the wedding. Most out-of-town groomsmen may have to fly out early the next morning which does not give them time to return their rented clothing. In some cases, return duties fall to the mother of the groom.

In my top package, I offer a great service of returning all the tuxedos. I learned a few lessons about returning tuxedos and suits through trial and error. I used to tell the guys to bring a set of clothes to change into right after the wedding and then hand me their rented items. After a late wedding at Houmas House, I collected all but one of the tuxedos and waited patiently on the porch of the bridal cottage until 2:00 a.m. for the last tuxedo. Unbeknownst to me, the stray groomsman was passed out in a field somewhere on the grounds. That night I created a new policy. I now pick up the tuxedos the next day at a designated hotel. I tell each groomsman if his tuxedo is not at the hotel by a certain time, he assumes the responsibility for returning it. I also inform the groomsmen that I am just the delivery girl. They are responsible for ensuring all items are in the tuxedo bag. I won't play "mom" and check the bags for them.

Since then, I've had no more mishaps regarding returns.

PINNING ON THE BOUTONNIERES

In my wedding planning course, I make sure each student can practice pinning on boutonnieres. They quickly learn that it is not as easy as it looks. Each student may try several times and still not get it right.

Here's the trick to pinning a bout: place it on the left side of the jacket (over the heart) and slightly tilt it to match the slant of the lapel. Lift the lapel and pin the bout from the back side onto the strongest part of the stem. The pin should point down and not be visible from the front. The bout should be sturdy, not floppy.

After years of practice, I can do it in a flash. Groomsmen marvel at how quickly I can pin, and they respond with "Wow, you've done this before!"

Yep. I've been pinning boutonnieres for more than twenty years.

Planning Tips

For your wedding gown and bridesmaid dresses:

1. Order your wedding gown with months to spare to allow time for alterations and your bridal portrait session if that's on your list of things to do.

2. Dresses for bridesmaids, the mother of the bride, and the mother of the groom should be ordered six months ahead of time.

3. Wear the appropriate underwear and shoes when trying on wedding gowns and bridesmaids' dresses and again when going for alterations.

4. Choose a gown style that looks fabulous on you and coordinates well with the theme of your venue and the weather.

5. Don't allow the opinions/criticism of others to spoil your gown-buying experience. Go shopping with just one other person. If you must bring an entourage, narrow your choices down to three dresses beforehand. That way, they'll have fewer dresses to pick apart and you'll end up with something you already know you like.

6. Take a similar approach to bridesmaids' dresses to avoid confusion and argument over style and color. Choose three dresses you like and let your bridesmaids choose from those.

7. Don't pay attention to size labels. Buy a gown that fits and flatters. Period.

For menswear:

1. Order tuxedos or suits six to eight months before the wedding day.

2. Dads and usher's ties, vests and cummerbunds can be a neutral color.

3. Tuxedos and suits can be picked up the day before the wedding and returned the day after the wedding.

4. Make sure each guy tries on his entire outfit before leaving the store.

5. For a two or three buttoned tuxedo or suit the bottom button is always left open.

Secret Confession

ALL IN A DAY'S WORK

Warning. The following story may make you blush.

As part of my service, I help the bride get dressed. That means I typically see my brides with few or no clothes on. No biggy. They don't have anything I haven't seen before. Every weekend as a bride steps into her wedding dress, a naked butt comes close to my face. I've had to tape boobs in place many times to ensure they fit perfectly into the dress. Hey, it's all in a day's work for a wedding planner!

Just a few weeks ago, my assistant Jill shared a story from a wedding she had helped with. "You're not going to believe what I had to do for the bride."

"Oh?" I asked, not particularly curious. After twenty years, I'd seen pretty much everything.

"The bride was sweating in her wedding gown—you know, the huge ballgown with layers and layers of crinoline."

I nodded, picturing the dress Jill referred to. "I can imagine how hot she must have been," I replied. Crinoline feels almost like a plastic netting, and in south Louisiana where it's always hot and humid, sweating is a no-brainer.

"Well," Jill continued, "the bride told me she needed someone to fan her, so I picked up a stack of papers and fanned her face and shoulders."

"Good," I said, wondering where this was going.

"This is where it gets really good," Jill said. "The bride said 'No, no! Not there. Under my dress.'"

"UNDER her dress?" I asked.

"Yes. And guess what happened then?"

"She held up her skirts?"

"Sort of. She hiked up her dress and sat down and I had to fan… her…her vagina!"

I burst into hysterical laughter. Jill told me she sat across from the bride and fanned her lower region for about twenty minutes, trying to look anywhere but straight ahead.

All in a day's work.

I can't begin to tell you how many brides I've escorted to the bathroom to help them pee. From holding up the dress, to holding the bride, to running water because they're too nervous to pee, to even wiping them. Yes, wiping the bride.

One of my past students, my dear friend Janine, told me that one time she had to assist a bride in changing her clothes for her departure. The bride had passed out from drinking too much and lay completely naked on the couch. Janine and the brand-new husband tried to sober her up and dress her while she was unconscious!

Janine ran into the bride the next day, and the bride turned bright red from embarrassment. Obviously, the groom had told her what transpired the night before.

We wedding planners have seen it all, done it all—and wow, we sure are troopers!

A GUIDE TO VENDORS

As you'll discover reading through this chapter, brides must deal with numerous vendors in preparation for her wedding. While some wedding planners will contract vendors on her behalf, I prefer the bride contract vendors directly, sign the contracts, and pay them. I am happy to hand the vendors their checks, but I won't issue payment from my account.

It's important to know who you are dealing with before you sign any contracts. Several years ago, a wedding planner convinced her bride to let her manage all the vendors on the bride's behalf. The wedding planner would arrange all contracts, all communications, and put down vendor deposits which the bride's family would pay to her in advance.

As the wedding approached, the mother of the bride had a question for the florist that required an immediate answer. When she could not reach the wedding planner for assistance, she called the florist directly. The florist told her that her daughter's wedding had not been contracted. It wasn't on her calendar. The mother panicked. She began calling all the vendors, and one by one each of them told her that they had not been contracted to serve her daughter's wedding—the venue, the band, everyone. The bride's family had handed thousands of dollars in vendor deposits to the wedding planner and she vanished.

A few weeks later, an investigative team knocked on their door and told them the wedding planner was in jail for check fraud. Surprise! Three months after this horrible debacle, the swindled bride hired me to pick up the pieces. I felt terrible for her. In the end, she had a lovely wedding and learned an important lesson about trust.

A caterer I frequently work with, Caryn Roland of Heirloom Cuisine, says, "Hire the vendors you can trust and trust the vendors you hire. Give us your ideas, wishes, and desires and then let us do our job. You will get much more by being polite and gracious than snotty and condescending. And above all, you get what you pay for."

It's a good strategic move for a bride to hire vendors who have worked together before and who like working with each other. When your vendors get along, they will enjoy their time serving you as well. That will truly make a huge difference in your entire day.

THE OFFICIANT

You cannot have a wedding without an officiant, yet sometimes the officiant is the last vendor brides think to hire. Book your officiant early. Without one, there is no wedding.

Start by deciding whether you want a judge, a minister, or a non-denominational person officiating your wedding. It may be helpful to watch video clips of some of the weddings your potential officiant has performed. If you're getting married in a church, you'll likely be expected to use the services of a priest or pastor affiliated with that church. If you want someone outside of the church to marry you, you must obtain the church's approval.

Sarah Corie of Eye Dew Weddings, an officiant and a dear friend of mine, told me that one of the most important pieces of advice she can give is to make sure the officiant properly pronounces the names of the bride, groom, and any family members mentioned in the service.

It's vitally important. In her first year of officiating weddings, one bride and groom each had interesting last names: Hunerjager and Loudenslager. "I practiced for weeks to make sure I said them correctly," she tells me. "I will always be grateful for the Hunerjager/ Loudenslager ceremony that taught me the importance of knowing how to pronounce my couple names correctly." She adds, "Yes, I have written permission to use their names!"

CEREMONY MUSICIANS

If the ceremony is at a church, refer to their guidelines before hiring anyone to perform music at your wedding. Sometimes churches only allow their own organist or other musicians including vocalists to perform at weddings. If your ceremony doesn't take place at a church, your options are wide open. From a string quartet, harp, guitar, or even an acapella choir, what you choose depends upon your preference. You may even want a DJ for your ceremony to ensure you hear the original music. For example, the Hallelujah Chorus is commonly recognized as an orchestral piece. It will sound quite different if it's played on the piano.

The number of songs played during a ceremony can vary, but there are typically several. Usually three or four pieces of prelude music are played as guests enter. Another song will accompany the entry of grandparents and parents. The music changes again as the bridal party enters, and of course, a special piece of music will accompany the bride as she walks down the aisle. During the ceremony, there may be a song for candle lighting or communion. Other music will play for the bridal party recessional and for the postlude as guests exit.

Remember, some songs are taboo in church. The traditional *Wedding March*, more commonly referred to as *Here Comes the Bride*, is not permitted in the Catholic Church. It's considered a secular song. Be careful and check with your church before choosing any music.

Some ceremony musicians may charge by the number of songs they are asked to play, while others may charge you according to the length of time they play. At a Catholic ceremony, prelude music can last twenty minutes. Add one-and-a-half hours for the ceremony and postlude.

At some of the venues I've used the ceremony and cocktail hour are held in one place. For a fee, ceremony musicians will extend their play time into the cocktail hour. It's nice to have background music playing during this time if your musicians and budget are willing.

THE FLORIST

I have never seen an ugly flower, have you? Unfortunately, I have seen the somewhat ugly look of disappointment on a bride's face when her bouquets are delivered and are not what she envisioned.

That is a sign of sheer miscommunication.

What a bride sees on Pinterest and what her budget will allow can be two totally different things. Make sure to communicate well with your florist. Pictures help tremendously. Swatches of your fabric colors are a great gauge as well.

Milissa Duhe of Designs by Milissa says she discovers a bride's style by asking her to describe her dress. The bride may respond that her dress is vintage, classic, and simple. Or she may describe her dress as funky, edgy, and fun. This simple unique approach gives Milissa a clearer vision of what the bride may want to see in her floral package.

In her initial meeting with a wedding client, Milissa also asks the bride to describe her dream wedding, budget aside. She takes careful notes, and then together they review the bride's vision to determine what can be eliminated according to her budget. Eighty bows on the pews may not be necessary for a or thirty-minute ceremony. It all comes down to budget.

Use visual comparisons to describe the bouquet or arrangement sizes you envision. For example, your arrangement can be as large as a charger plate, a dinner plate, or a bread plate. Anything that will give your florist a vivid impression of the size you have in mind.

For one wedding in an enormous cathedral, the florist delivered two large arrangements for the altar area. Although the arrangements were sizeable, they were dwarfed by the enormous altar next to them. The mother of the bride gasped in horror and began sobbing when she saw them. I called the florist, who had already left. The florist told me the size described was what they delivered, and it was a size that fit the bride's budget. I encouraged her to send someone back to adjust the arrangements and make the mother of the bride happy. She did!

That experience was a huge lesson for me. I now tell my clients to be super meticulous when describing size and color. Sometimes the color of the shipped flowers varies slightly from what you envisioned. Mother Nature is a free-spirited creator. Any difference in growing conditions or seed variety can impact the color or its intensity. The florist should make this clear and stipulate the possibility in their contract. Just be forewarned.

Most florists request a deposit up front and need the balance paid as much as two months before the wedding so they can order the flowers.

THE DESIGNER

Don't confuse the designer with the florist! A designer is typically hired for a venue that needs to be transformed from head to toe. He or she creates the mood, style, and ambiance for the ceremony and reception. They can transform tents into stately ballroom through décor by draping chiffon over ugly walls, hanging chandeliers, and suggesting floral arrangements to enhance the space. For more on selecting a designer, see Chapter 2, "Getting Professional Help."

THE CATERER

Some wedding venues provide mandatory in-house catering while other venues allow you to use the services of an outside caterer.

If you hire a caterer, choosing the right one is crucial. If the food is bad or even just so-so, your guests will remember. Your guests will remember if the food is fabulous too. Years after the wedding, they'll still be talking about the delectable bacon-wrapped shrimp or that tender juicy brisket or the spicy blackened catfish. (Now my mouth is watering!)

Of course, serving high quality food makes common sense, but it directly impacts your budget. The more guests you have, the more you'll pay for food. Know your food budget before you hire a caterer or determine your menu.

Food tends to be easier on the budget in the South where we are used to buffet style receptions that require fewer serving personnel. Almost everywhere else, receptions include a sit-down dinner which is an obviously higher expense.

Begin your search for a caterer by asking friends and family who they have used in the past and who's food they absolutely loved. Or attend bridal shows where caterers offer food samples. If you like what you taste, set up an appointment. Did you know that some restaurants offer outside catering? The amazing Mexican restaurant that you and your fiancé love could possibly be your caterer.

Once you've determined your guest count and your budget, start setting up your appointments with caterers that pique your interest. Not all caterers offer tastings. For those who don't, be sure to get referrals. Check their website and social media for reviews and ask around to see if their food is up to snuff.

Let's say you've narrowed it down to three caterers. Now it's time to check out their menus and pricing. Some important questions to ask a caterer are:

1. What is your server to guest ratio? This is essential. To save money, some caterers will only hire a small staff who then must rush around to keep up with bussing tables or serving guests.

2. Will you provide plates, cutlery, and napkins?

3. What will your staff wear at the reception? (If you have an ultra-formal wedding, you may not want the staff to be wearing jeans and polo shirts.)

4. Have you ever catered at my venue before, and are you familiar with their rules and regulations? (For example, we hold numerous weddings at historical buildings in Louisiana, such as the Old Governor's Mansion and Louisiana's Old State Capital. Both forbid red wine and open flames.)

5. Are there any additional costs such as gratuity fees, service charges, clean up fees, and so on?

6. Do you charge extra to cut the cake? (Surprisingly, some caterers do.)

7. Do you offer vegetarian, vegan, gluten free or dairy-free options?

8. Is the menu fixed or can it be customized?

9. Are any rentals included with the catering fee such as tables or linens for the food and service tables?

10. Do you offer bar service? (See the next section for more on bar service.)

11. Who will be the point person on the wedding day?

When you receive your proposal or contract, read it through multiple times. Know exactly what you're getting. You don't want any surprises popping up on your wedding day.

Communicating well with your caterer is essential for a successful reception. The words of Caryn are worth repeating. "Hire the vendors you can trust and trust the vendors you hire. Give us your ideas, wishes and desires and then let us do our job. You will get much more by being polite and gracious than snotty and condescending. And above all, you get what you pay for."

Now for the biggest challenge faced by every bride, mother of the bride, and father of the bride: how to figure out what number of guests to give your caterer for the final count. Most caterers like to have the final count four to two weeks before the wedding. The first rule of thumb is to always start with a lower number. You can always go higher but it's difficult to go lower once you lock yourself in with a contract. Remember that some of the guests who say they will attend may end up with a sick child or another emergency and be unable to come. The general rule is eighty to eighty-five percent of your total number of invited guests will attend. Say you are inviting 180 guests. You can expect to receive between 144 and 153 guests. You don't want to pay for people who don't show, but you don't want to run out of food either. Try to get as close as you can.

What if some surprise guests show up and you end up with 190, not 153? Don't be shocked if the caterer comes to you that night and asks for payment for the extra thirty-seven guests. And honestly, that's what you want! You want to pay for guests who attend, not for guests who don't show. Be aware that some caterers may charge you a penalty if more people show up than you contracted them to serve. Check with them about their policy prior to the wedding.

If you're serving guests buffet style, chances are some food will be leftover. Delegate someone ahead of time to home those leftovers and refrigerate them.

THE BAR

Remembering your budget, determine what kind of alcohol you'll serve. Are you sticking with beer and wine? Adding in champagne and a signature drink? Or will you offer a full open bar?

Many caterers offer bar service with their menus. They may charge per person or by consumption. Louisiana tends to have an abundance of heavy drinkers, so I always suggest go by a per person price. Caterers have bar service down to a science. If you're fortunate enough to have the option to pay per person, you won't have to figure anything out. Your vendor will set up the entire bar with ice, glassware, and all the mixers and garnishes—plus they'll know exactly how much to bring depending on your final count.

It's always a good idea to keep your bar simple. Unless you hire several bartenders, serving mojitos or Bloody Marys with all the fixings will take time. The line to the bar will grow long, and your guests will become frustrated. Sticking with beer, wine, champagne, and mixed drinks—along with non-alcoholic selections of water, soft drinks, and iced tea—is a more practical option. If you choose to serve a fancy signature drink, the bartenders can make gallons ahead of time for faster service. Depending on your budget, you can select premium liquors, top-shelf, or mid-priced liquor.

Being conscientious about your tipsy guests can save you some money in the long run. If you shut down the bar for the last hour of your reception serving only water and possibly coffee, you'll give your guests time to sober up before they get behind the wheel. Otherwise, consider providing shuttle services or reminding your guests to use Uber or Lyft.

THE BAKERY

I'm not a wedding cake expert and I certainly don't bake them, but I have cut and served over a thousand in my lifetime. I've seen enough of these elaborate works of art to offer a few suggestions.

When choosing your wedding cake, select a design that coordinates with the theme and style of your wedding. Whether your wedding is classic or vintage or edgy, it's a nice touch when your wedding cake follows suit.

If your wedding is taking place in Louisiana, you may want to order a groom's cake too. If you're not familiar with the concept of a groom's cake, it's based on a tradition that began in Victorian England. Because the official wedding cake was considered too fancy for the groom, he had one of his own. The tradition found its way to the American South where it is still alive and well.

Groom's cakes are usually decadent chocolate decorated in fondant. They can be amazing works of art in all kinds of different shapes and sizes. Some may look like Ambrosia Bakery's famous LSU football stadium cakes, while others might be shaped like wine bottles or whisky barrels. Other times, they may be simpler—chocolate cake covered with chocolate-dipped strawberries.

People often ask, "Allie, how much cake do I need?" I can happily answer that question. If you're hosting a get together the day after the wedding, leftover cake comes in handy. If not, it's usually wasted. A general rule of thumb is to order enough wedding cake to serve two-thirds of your attending guests—even if you wish to save the top of the cake for an anniversary celebration. Your heart may palpitate in fear of running out, but in my years of serving wedding cake, that's never happened. We have tons of leftover cake at almost every wedding. If you're ordering a groom's cake too, order enough of it to serve one third of your guest count.

Wedding guests who drink heavily typically bypass the wedding cake altogether. It goes the other way as well. If your guests don't imbibe heavily or if you choose not to serve alcohol, they will devour the wedding cake. Keep that in mind when placing your order.

If you happen to be on a tight budget, there is nothing wrong with ordering a smaller cake as a décor item and a sheet cake to be cut in the kitchen and served to the guests. No one will think twice about whether the slice on their plate came from the cake on display. Many of my brides have used dummy layers in cake tiers to make the overall presentation grander in size. (As their wedding planner, when it came time to cutting the cake for the camera, I discreetly remind the couple to not cut the dummy layer!)

It's always good to have the cake on some type of cake plateau or riser to elevate the cake from the table for a beautiful presentation. I keep an array of plateaus in my vehicle just in case the bakery forgets to bring the plateau or the bride forgot to order one. If you have your own plateau, make sure to ask the bakery the measurements of the base layer of the cake to ensure your plateau is large enough. If the bottom layer is eighteen inches, your plateau needs to be at least twenty inches in diameter.

THE CAKE TABLE

Some venues automatically provide cake tables for weddings and include a simple linen covering or even a specialty linen, but it's always worth checking into. Making assumptions with any aspect of wedding planning is always a bad idea. In some cases, you'll have to make sure you have all the necessary items for the cake table yourself or have your planner do it for you.

In the South, we usually invite the entire bridal party to surround the cake table for an informal toast to the bride and groom with champagne and champagne glasses. This is more of a photo opportunity than a real toast, but it can make a lovely picture for your album. If you plan to do this, check with your venue or caterer to make sure there are enough champagne flutes available for your bridal party.

Before the reception begins, set up the cake table with the bride and groom's special champagne flutes, cake knife and server, and a plate with some napkins and two forks, just in case you don't want to use your fingers to feed each other. Make sure your caterer or venue supplies the cake plates, forks, and napkins. If they don't, you will need to remember supply them yourself or ask your planner to do it for you.

CAKE SERVICE

After you and your new husband have completed the formalities of cutting the cake and feeding each other for the photographer, it's time for the rest of the cake to be cut and served to your guests.

That leads to a hidden cost that many people are unaware of. Some caterers charge extra to cut and serve the cake. I don't recommend saving money by inviting your great aunt Suzie to cut your cake for you unless she's a professional wedding cake cutter. Otherwise she may create a mess on the cake table.

The best approach to cake cutting is to disassemble the layers. Cut the large bottom layer first and work your way up. If smaller layers are cut first, you may end up carrying home a large portion of that twenty-two-inch, ten-pound, base layer. If you have leftovers, it's much easier to wrap and transfer a smaller layer.

Challenges to this approach arise when each cake layer has a different filling. Guests may request the strawberry and cream in the smallest layer instead of the lemon butter cream in the large base layer. In that case, both layers are cut. If you want multiple flavors, it makes sense to anticipate the most popular flavor and use it for the largest layer.

An old wives' tale suggests that if a single woman places a slice of wedding cake under her pillow, she will dream of the man she will marry. I'm not sure if people do that anymore, but I do know that some people love to snack on wedding cake post-wedding. Make sure to order some cake bags in case guests want to take an extra piece home with them.

For wrapping leftover cake, I usually bring aluminum foil and plastic wrap. Place the anniversary top in a box and then tightly wind several layers of plastic wrap around the box to help reduce freezer burn. Be aware that some bakeries require the return of cake hardware such as cake plateaus and any dividers or dowels in the cake. Check their requirements ahead of time, and make sure the cake cutter is aware. Otherwise you may be slapped with a charge for not returning those pieces.

I make sure the bride and groom have several slices of cake in a box to take to their hotel room. Often the couple doesn't have a chance to eat a piece of their own painstakingly chosen cake. I also make sure parents of the bride and groom have some cake to take as well in case they were too busy to stop and enjoy a piece. As their wedding planner, it's my job to be conscientious of their needs and to provide top notch service.

One last piece of advice. Make sure to delegate taking home all the leftover food and cake to someone who has the capability to refrigerate it.

THE BAND OR DJ

Once you've gone to all the trouble of choosing a band or DJ for your wedding, take good care of them and their equipment. Ask what they need to make their evening efficient, effective, and fun. This is particularly important if your reception is being held outside. Give them a stage under an enclosed, climate-controlled tent with heaters and air conditioning.

Mary from the band Rewind says, "Especially avoid putting your band outside in the freezing cold. It negatively affects instrument tuning, damages equipment, and makes it hard for the musicians to feel and move their fingers to play their instruments. The band will sound bad under those conditions. It's inevitable. And if your band is uncomfortable, your guests will be too and will likely want to leave early. Indoors is always the safer bet!" Wise words indeed.

Mary also suggests, "Before you book your venue, check to make sure the acoustics and electricity are good. Ask your band about the venue you are considering if you're not sure about the acoustics. A loud and boomy room will hurt your guests' ears, among other issues. Hire an electrician to ensure the band has enough good clean, dedicated power five feet or less away from the stage—important—especially for outdoor receptions or receptions at a private home. Without proper electricity, you'll have no music."

One last suggestion from Mary: "Trust that your band knows what they are doing. Don't try to control every aspect of the music or when each song should be played. Also, avoid requesting a bunch of obscure songs nobody knows. You might love those songs, but your guests probably won't get it and it might clear the dance floor. But if that's not something you care about, then go for it! Put in your requests and let the band decide what will work best and what won't. They are the experts. Trust them."

My final piece of guidance for you regarding music is to hire a versatile band that can appeal to all ages. Your guests will appreciate a variety of music, so look for a group that can cater to different eras and genres.

DANCING

Choreographed first dances tend to look stiff and unnatural. Don't take dance lessons specifically for your wedding unless you can effortlessly master the steps. Remember, it's okay if you don't dance like the contestants on Dancing with the Stars. Nobody expects you to. An uncomfortable effort only makes you look mechanical. Generally, guests pay little attention to the first dance or the father/daughter and mother/son dances. Save your money and put it elsewhere. On the other hand, comical style first dances can be very entertaining and go over well. If that's your speed, go for it! Your guests will love it.

Bridal party dances are usually the most awkward dance of the evening. Spare everyone the pain and skip it unless you're designing it as an entertainment feature.

After a reception, people remember the aspects of it that made them feel good like the great food, the atmosphere, and the good time they had. If the reception wasn't entertaining, they won't remember it. If the food was terrible, they will remember it negatively. The ambience of the room is also important. It's worth investing money in excellent food, a warm atmosphere, and an interactive band to stir up the party if you want your reception to be awesome and memorable.

A GUIDE TO TIPPING

Who should the bride tip? This is the million-dollar question. At one wedding, the mother of the bride had a tip for everyone involved in the wedding, and I mean EVERYONE! From each vendor to each server, bus boy, bartender, bar back, and valet, right down to the dishwasher. Yes, even the dishwasher. I was impressed and in awe. I had never seen this happen, and I'm not sure I'll ever see it again. The mother of the bride had a stack of envelopes for me to hand out, each one addressed with the recipient's title.

You should have seen the expressions that appeared as I presented those envelopes one by one—especially from individuals who don't normally receive tips or even acknowledgement. They were shocked. I felt like I was Santa Claus or maybe even Oprah. It was a wonderful feeling to say the least. Even I was included! Woo-hoo!

We vendors love getting tips. In the South, it's what we call a wonderful "lagniappe," (a little something extra) and it makes us feel as though we did a good job. You wouldn't tip someone who didn't do a good job, would you?

Sometimes, however, the bride is on a tight budget. Does she have to tip? In my opinion, no. It is not mandatory. It is mandatory to tip a server when you go out to eat though, at least twenty percent. Is tipping your vendors a nice gesture? Of course it is. But once again, it is not mandatory.

There are other ways you can show your appreciation for a great job. A hand-written note is always welcome. Let each vendor know how much you appreciated their hard work at your wedding or how they made it special or so much fun. Whenever I receive a thank you note from one of my brides, I display it in my office as proudly as if it were from one of my kids. It means a lot to be thanked and acknowledged.

Writing a great review on a vendor's website or on other sites like The Knot Worldwide is a terrific way to show your appreciation. Positive reviews help us get more bookings. Please write them! Another great way to thank vendors as opposed to tipping them is to give them a great big shout out on social media. Use all forms of social media. Tag them and hashtag the name of their business. I promise you that effort will be greatly appreciated.

If you have the resources to leave a monetary tip, here are a few guidelines to determine how much to give:

- ► **Hair and Makeup:** Fifteen to twenty percent is typical, just like a salon, but it's not mandatory.

- ► **Officiant:** They should charge a fee. If not, you should "gift" them with some money, usually between $300 and $500. If they won't accept it, donate the money to the church.

- ► **Catering:** Most catering contracts include a gratuity charge, but you can still slip each server and bartender a twenty. Find out in advance how many servers and bartenders will be at your wedding.

- ► **Wedding Planners, Coordinators, Designers, and Decorators:** I never really expect a tip but when I get one, I'm grateful for it. Ten to twenty percent is plenty to say, "Thank you for making my wedding great."

- ► **Band:** When the band has ten members or more, it can get pretty costly to tip them. Standard tips are usually $20 to $50 per band member.

- ▶ **DJ:** Ten to twenty percent of the cost of the DJ services is a typical tip rate. Remember, these guys have to lug all that heavy equipment to the ceremony and reception sites.

- ▶ **Florist:** They usually never get tipped but if you can, ten to twenty percent is great.

- ▶ **Photographer and Videographer:** This is difficult for some brides who may not feel comfortable tipping until they see the finished product. However, if these professionals did an exceptional job on your wedding day, were helpful, and had a tremendous attitude, you can tip them fifteen to twenty percent of their price.

- ▶ **Transportation:** Ten to twenty percent for each driver is a great way to say thank you—even if the contract says the gratuity is included in the price. If the driver goes above and beyond expectations, by all means tip him or her.

VENDORS SUMMARY

In summary, it's always best to hire the vendors you trust, and to then trust the vendors you hire. Take your vendors' lead and seriously consider any suggestions they offer. For example, as a wedding planner, I highly recommend you and your groom take a private dining moment before entering the reception. It will be a highlight of your wedding day.

Do remember that any vendor can only provide so much on your budget. It's not their fault if the budget is tight and you can't have exactly what you want. It sounds simple, but people sometimes forget that you get what you pay for. And don't forget to be polite and gracious toward everyone you work with. You'll get greater service than you would receive by being snotty and condescending. I'm shocked at how many times delightful vendors have been treated badly by brides and family. It shouldn't happen, but it does.

There is a misconception that all businesses should separate personal and professional lives, but in the wedding industry it just isn't feasible because of the hours we keep. Therefore, if you want to meet after hours or on weekends, your vendor may have to bring their kids along. If you don't like that, look for another vendor. One vendor told me that when her kids were young, she would occasionally meet brides at Chuck E Cheese. If you want flexibility from your vendors, you will need to be flexible too.

Give us your ideas, wishes, hopes, and dreams, and then let us do our job. Most of all, have fun. Planning your wedding should be enjoyable, so hire people who make it as exciting as it should be.

Wedding Planner Tips

1. Review the sections about individual vendors before you speak with them to remind yourself of specific details to consider.

2. Be sure to ask vendors questions about every aspect of their service and ask for references or examples. (Take special note of the section on caterers; there are plenty of questions to ask to receive good food service within your budget.)

3. Consider how much time each vendor will allot to your wedding, details about what they offer you during that time, and how much it would cost should things extend beyond expectations or run longer than expected.

4. Ask what the vendors need and expect from you to allow your wedding to flow smoothly.

5. Find out who your contact person will be.

6. If possible, hire vendors who have worked together before. It makes the day go more smoothly.

Secret Confession

A STREETCAR NAMED "LOST"

My beloved New Orleans is a fascinating city full of personality and ambiance. But it is a tangled beast to move around in. At a recent wedding, the bride and bridesmaids were having their hair and makeup done at the beautiful Omni Royal Hotel in the heart of the French Quarter. For this wedding, the bride had contracted the only trolley remaining on her wedding date to transport her, her bridesmaids, and family to the ceremony. The trolley was a couple of hours outside of New Orleans.

The ceremony was scheduled for 7:00 p.m. at a church in Metairie, which is about a twenty-five-minute drive from the hotel in good traffic. However, traffic is unpredictable in New Orleans because the city often has a million activities underway at the same time. For that reason, the bride engaged a police escort as New Orleans brides are encouraged to do. A police escort can stop traffic quickly, pull the wedding vehicles through, and get everyone to the church or reception on time.

The trolley was scheduled to arrive at 6:00 p.m. Now here's the glitch: an Italian American parade was booked to come down the street at the same time, slowing down all traffic coming to and from the hotel. But the trolley owner told me the trolley would leave for the hotel at 2:00 p.m., providing a four-hour window. That seemed like plenty of time.

As always, I confirmed each vendor on the week of the wedding including the trolley company. No problems. Everything was under control.

On the wedding day, the trolley driver contacted me at about 5:15 p.m. "I'm in the city."

"That's great!" I said, glad that we had arranged that four-hour window. "Where are you?"

"I don't know."

"Tell me the name of the street you're on."

"I don't know."

My stomach sank. "Okay, are you using your GPS?"

"Yes ma'am," he replied.

"Okay, what street does it say are you on?"

"It doesn't say." I detected a note of panic in his voice.

I took a deep breath to swallow my alarm. "Alright then. Take a look out your window for a street sign."

Finally, he was able to tell me where he was—on the opposite end of town from the hotel! With all the streets blocked by the Italian parade, he got turned around. Apparently, he was not familiar enough with the city to find his way out of the tangle—even with his GPS.

The father of the bride overheard my conversation and asked to speak with the trolley driver. "I live here. I know this city like the back of my hand," he said helpfully.

I handed him the phone and watched frustration grow on his face as he spoke with the completely lost and disoriented driver. He got no further than I had.

I approached our police escorts on their motorcycles.

"Our trolley is lost. Can you please speak to the driver and help him?"

"Yes ma'am." One officer took the phone and tried to reel in the trolley driver.

A few minutes passed. The officer's voice rose, and frustration pinched his face. I glanced at my watch. It was 6:15 p.m. The trolley was now fifteen minutes late. Timing was particularly critical because the ceremony was taking place at a Catholic church where time was stringently adhered to. On top of that, the Archbishop was presiding. If you were fifteen minutes late, the rules said they would cut out the full mass. If you were later than that, they could choose to cancel the ceremony.

I took the phone back from the police officer. It was now 6:25 p.m. The trolley driver was still lost and frantic, we were surrounded on every side by a parade of loud music and noisy celebrating people, and the ceremony was scheduled to start at 7:00 pm.

I approached the police escorts again. "Do you fellows think you might be able to go and find the lost trolley?" I asked.

The officer who had tried to coax the trolley driver in the right direction shook his head. "We don't do that."

I looked at the other officer. "We're really in a bind. The church may cancel the ceremony. Can you please help us and find him? Please. I'd do it myself, but there's no way I can get through traffic or roadblocks as easily as you can."

The second police officer sighed. "Okay." He turned to his partner. "Let's get it done." They hoped on their motorcycles and took off.

It was now 6:30 p.m. Even if the trolley magically appeared in five minutes, we'd make it to the church by the skin of our teeth.

My phone rang. It was the lost trolley driver again. They were on their way, but they were having trouble getting through the blocked traffic. Then one of the motorcycles got a flat tire, leaving only one escort.

Really? A flat tire. When does a cop ever get a flat tire? What next? The clock kept ticking. 6:35 p.m.

Finally, about fifteen minutes later, the blue lights of our single-officer police escort rounded the corner a few blocks away. I quickly led the bride and her entourage to the loading zone. When the trolley pulled in, they scurried on board and the trolley left. I hopped into my own car a block away and texted my assistant an update, asking her to text me when the trolley arrived.

Ping! Notification came at 7:05 p.m.

Thankfully, despite the chaos, this lovely couple had a full mass. They got married and the reception was fantastic!

A few days later, I heard the trolley company had refunded some of the payment. The mother of the bride said the best money she spent was on my services and the police escorts.

I'm happy to be of service.

HAIR AND MAKEUP

T he beautiful bride gliding down the aisle toward her groom doesn't appear the way she does because some fairy godmother waved a magic wand. It took time and patience for her to find the right dress, the right shoes, and the right flowers. Obviously, preparations didn't stop there. She also spent significant time on hair and makeup.

The most important stress-minimizing tip I can offer brides for their wedding day is to schedule enough time for hair and makeup. In fact, schedule MORE time than you think you'll need, because it always takes more time than you might expect. ALWAYS. I can honestly say that in my experience, running behind is almost always due to delays in the beauty preparation department.

In my world of weddings, brides are usually accompanied by an average of six to eight bridesmaids. With the bride, that makes seven to nine people getting ready at the same time. Add the mother of the bride, the mother of the groom, the possibility of grandmothers, junior bridesmaids, and perhaps a flower girl or two, and the number of females getting ready can easily grow to a dozen people or more. Scheduling can become a nightmare simply due to the number of people involved. Of course, how much time you need will depend upon whether each person is doing their own hair and makeup or if you are hiring professionals.

DIY HAIR OR MAKEUP PROFESSIONAL?

Often, bridesmaids are expected to pay for their own hair styling and makeup. For that reason, some brides accept the do-it-yourself approach to respect their bridesmaid's pocketbooks. Sometimes, the bride pays for professional hair and makeup services as part of a bridal party gift.

Using professionals to style hair and apply makeup for the entire bridal party does create a more unified look. The effect of the bride and her entourage wearing similar hair styles, the same color palette for blush, eyeshadow, and lip gloss—and for the bridesmaids' dresses—is stunning. On the other hand, allowing everyone to do their own thing is a more spontaneous approach that shows great individuality.

There is no right or wrong approach, however. Don't stress! It's all about the look you ultimately want to achieve. Whether you choose DIY or professional, the important thing to remember is that once hair and makeup are completed, everyone will look beautiful. The memories you create for your special day are what will last.

SCHEDULING

How do you determine how much time you'll need? It depends upon the approach you're taking.

If each person is doing their own hair and makeup, plan for forty-five minutes, total, for each person. That will give you plenty of time to enjoy each other's company as you get ready.

If you're hiring professionals, it will take longer, because you'll usually have one makeup artist and one hairdresser taking care of everyone. Most makeup artists and hairdressers I have worked with are independent and work solo. There are a few companies out there who might send more than one makeup artist or stylist, but usually it's just one person.

The process unfolds in staggered assembly-line fashion. For example, one person's hair will be rolled, then the next, and so on. When the stylist gets to the end of the line, he or she will return to the first person to comb and style. The makeup artist does her work between rolling and styling.

I block off at least two hours for the bride's hair and makeup and an hour for each other person. That may seem like a lot of time, but on a wedding day, time is slippery. People are less focused and conversation wanders. Excitement peppers the air and makes activities feel scattered. What may take ten minutes on a "normal" day may take triple the time on a wedding day. So, if you happen to have six bridesmaids, two mothers, a grandmother and the bride, that's ten people and eleven hours. Yes, you read that correctly: eleven hours.

The bride should never be first or last with hair or makeup. She wouldn't want to be polished and perfect by 10:00 a.m. if the ceremony doesn't begin until 6:00 p.m. On the other hand, she wouldn't want to be the last one in the chair worrying about whether or not she'll be ready on time. Preferably, the bride should have her hair done somewhere between halfway or two thirds of the way through the session.

For similar reasons, the mother of the bride should not be first or last either. It's crucial for her to be ready and fully dressed ahead of the bride so she can help the bride dress and prepare for any pre-ceremony photographs.

Now, let's throw a wrench into the system with the new "first look" tradition. If the bride and groom are meeting before the ceremony to have their pictures taken, the timeline will need to begin even earlier. Typically, the first look happens about two hours before the ceremony. That means hair and makeup could begin as early as 6:00 or 7:00 a.m.

One way to ensure hair and makeup is done in a timely manner is to use a reputable individual or company. Nothing makes me more nervous than when a bride tells me her friend is excellent at applying makeup or doing hair. Although it's great to have friends involved in your special day, remember they are not professionals. You can't blame them when they aren't prepared to manage the unexpected. Using a seasoned, experienced hair and makeup professional or team ensures timeliness and precision.

DON'T FORGET A TRIAL RUN

Scheduling a trial run for your hair and makeup before the wedding day can save you a lot of grief. If you've scheduled a pre-wedding portrait session, your trial run will happen at that time. If a pre-wedding portrait isn't on your list of things to do, you might consider trying out your hair and makeup as you prepare for one of your many parties or showers. That will give you a great feel for what you want—and perhaps what you don't want—in terms of the look you're trying to achieve. A trial run will give you time to tweak the look and make it perfect for your wedding day.

I have seen brides run to the bathroom in tears and wash off their makeup or tear their hair apart because they hated it so much. They ended up redoing everything on their own. Whenever this nightmare happened, it happened because the bride did not have a trial run.

Make sure you have a trial run, no matter what. Don't wait until the wedding day. You may regret it.

1. Decide whether you're going to go for DIY hair and makeup or hire professionals.

2. Schedule plenty of time for hair and makeup on the morning of the wedding—a two-hour minimum for brides and an hour for each other person.

3. Start early enough to accommodate a first look photo session if you have one scheduled.

4. Make sure to have a trial run of hair and makeup well ahead of the wedding so there is time to tweak anything you're unhappy with.

Secret Confession

"SHOULD I STAY, OR SHOULD I GO?"

One wedding that's seared into my memory took place at a Catholic Church early in my career, before I became a full-fledged wedding planner. The bride had made only one request of her groom for their wedding day: do not drink alcohol at all before the ceremony.

He said he wouldn't.

When the groom walked into the church that day, his vest was inside out, his bow tie hung loose around his neck, and his eyes were blurry red. He smiled like a Cheshire cat as he approached me. I immediately smelled alcohol on his breath.

I handed him a mint and approached the best man, incredulous. "Oh my gosh, what have you done?" I asked. "He promised his bride he wouldn't drink before the ceremony."

"There's no way I'm not going to not buy my buddy a drink before his wedding," the best man told me. They had spent most of the day in a bar.

During our early consultations, the bride and groom had decided to do a "first look," to see each other before the ceremony and have all their pictures taken then. It gives the photographer more time to take pictures and allows the bride and groom to join the reception and party right after the ceremony instead of taking a thirty-minute delay for pictures.

A first look is not easy with a drunken groom.

I tried to pull him together. I gave him water, adjusted his vest and bow tie, and held my breath as the bride walked into the sanctuary where they were taking their first pictures.

The bride took one look at him—one look—and she knew. "Oh my God!" she cried and ran to the bathroom. I followed her with my heart in my throat and watch as she flopped onto the toilet (lid down), sobbing, her dress all puffed up around her.

As tears ran down her face, she looked up. "What am I supposed to do?" she wailed. "I asked him one thing. ONE THING. And he couldn't do it! He obviously has a drinking problem, what should I do?"

It was difficult time for me to hear that question. I'd just been through a really rough divorce and was leery of any potential problems. My brain screamed a response: "RUN! RUN NOW! RUN LIKE HELL!" But I couldn't get the words out of my mouth.

"Should I stay, or should I go?" she asked, still sobbing.

Even though I was freaking out inside, I managed to keep a calm demeanor and tried to process the situation. I wasn't qualified to answer her questions. I wasn't a marriage counselor or a therapist, just a measly wedding coordinator. I had to be incredibly careful with my response because this could change the trajectory of her entire life. Talk about pressure. Although they had prepared me to expect the unexpected in my training, this was far beyond anything I could have imagined, and now I was now deep in the trenches with no escape.

Finally, some words came to mind, words I'd heard a long time ago and taken to heart even though I couldn't remember who said them. I crouched down to meet my bride eye to eye and placed my hands on her shoulders. "This is the time when you have to ask yourself an important question: what are you willing to live with, and what are you willing to live without? At this moment, you must make the choice, stand by it, and live with it."

"RUN! RUN LIKE HELL, WOMAN!" still roared through my brain, but I managed to wait calmly for her answer.

Believe it or not, she decided to live with his drinking problem and stand by her decision.

"Okay. You've made your decision," I said. "Now, let's get things rolling."

She dried her tears, touched up her makeup, walked out of the bathroom, and married her tipsy groom. They had a beautiful wedding and a wonderful, fun reception.

I'm sure the days, months, and years that followed were not always easy. I often wondered about her. A few years ago, I saw an Instagram post celebrating their 15th wedding anniversary! How awesome is that?

And to think, I almost told her to run. I'm glad I didn't.

PRE-CEREMONY
AND CEREMONY

T he wedding day pre-ceremony begins when hair and makeup begin. It lasts until the bride and her bridesmaids line up for the walk down the aisle. The whole process, from preparation to ceremony, involves several stages. Each stage invites a whole whirlwind of activities. While it's my job to manage those activities, they will unfold in smoother fashion if you know what's coming.

STAGE ONE: HAIR AND MAKEUP

If the bride has hired a package that includes a first look, I usually arrive at the site where hair and makeup are done about four hours before the ceremony or photograph session. (The groom and his entourage are generally on their own until the photographer's second shooter comes to take their pictures. Depending upon the package selected, an assistant might help keep them organized and on time.)

After I wish the bride a happy wedding day and see that she is settled, I steam the wedding gown and the veil. Then it's ready for the photographer who may want to take a photograph of the dress hanging in a window, archway, or corridor. Because it could end up in a photograph, it's a great idea to have a special attractive hanger to hold your wedding gown. If you don't have a special hanger, choose a wooden one rather than plastic.

Many photographers take pictures of the bride's personal items such as her rings, other jewelry, garters, a special perfume for the day, an invitation, a hankie, shoes, and the like. It's helpful to have all your accessories in one place. I place a reminder in the itinerary and invite the bride to consider providing a pretty box or bag to hold those items.

Once the bride's veil and dress are ready to go, I steam dresses for the bridesmaids, the mothers, and the flower girls, making sure their clothes are ready before their hair and makeup is finished.

Usually, steam time is peppered with calls from vendors who have last minute questions—just one more reason have a wedding planner or coordinator! If I'm fielding calls, it allows the mother of the bride to enjoy preparations with her daughter rather than worrying about where this vendor should park, or if it's okay to change the order of something in the schedule, or if it's alright for the florist to tweak the centerpieces, or if there is an extension available for the stage because it's too small for the band. That's what I'm there for; to answer all the questions and make executive decisions that would otherwise stress out the bride and her mother.

As I steam dresses, I keep a careful eye on the time and watch proceedings like a hawk. I follow every element of the itinerary closely, making sure the hair and makeup session is unfolding as planned and that the bride is tended to about halfway or two-thirds of the way through the process, not dead last. While I work, the bride is usually hanging out with her bridesmaids telling funny stories, reminiscing, and sipping on a mimosa.

This is what you want, people! You sure don't want the bride to be a bundle of anxiety because she's sitting in the chair last and running late while the photographer has started taking pictures of the wedding gown hanging and all the bridesmaid's dresses. The feeling that events are beginning without her would be overwhelming.

Sometimes brides and grooms will exchange gifts or letters or both. Before the chaos ensues, it's good to give the bride a quiet moment to read the letter and open her gift. You'll want to have this captured on video and get pictures of it as well.

Once everyone is finished with hair and makeup, we usually take a group picture of them wearing special robes or PJs that have been gifted to them by the bride—from flowered silk robes to pale pink PJs or monogramed, buttoned-down shirts. They always look beautiful!

STAGE TWO: GETTING DRESSED

Next, it's time for the bride and her entourage to get dressed. This can become quite chaotic. I always tell them to nail down decisions about their outfits ahead of time. The wedding day is NOT the day to try on various bras or shapewear or shoes with their dresses.

I'm usually on hand to zip, tie, and adjust the bridesmaid's dresses. All sorts of unexpected things can happen, including broken zippers. I once had to sew a bridesmaid into her dress! I'm ready for any emergency and always keep a box of hypoallergenic, double-sided Topstick tape in my emergency kit. Although it's designed to hold men's toupees, it also neatly secures girls' dresses along the bustline. When they bend down, nothing falls out of place. That tape has been used for all kinds of things like fixing hems in a pinch, taping a groomsmen's shoe together, fixing boutonnieres, and even sticking to heels to the backs of shoes to prevent blisters.

Once everyone else is dressed, we concentrate on the bride. I encourage brides to step into the gown to avoid messing up hair and makeup. If the gown absolutely must go over her head, it's helpful to have several people assist. As they open the top of the dress, the bride raises her arms above her head and presses her lips together to keep lipstick from touching the dress.

Twenty minutes is usually plenty for the bride to dress, but to be safe, I usually ask my brides how their wedding gown fastens. For instance, does it close with a zipper or lace, or does it button with those pesky loops? If fastening the gown will be a lengthy procedure, I add extra time to the itinerary. For example, a corset takes a long time to tie, so I'll block off an extra thirty minutes to accommodate it. That may sound like a long time to put a dress on, but remember, what might take ten minutes under typical circumstances can take thirty minutes on your wedding day. Time flies, but regular activities take three times as long. It's a strange phenomenon, one I'm still trying to figure out.

STAGE THREE: THE REVEAL

If the bridesmaids didn't help the bride dress, the bride will sometimes do a reveal for them once she's fully put together. Sometimes a bride will do a reveal for her dad. The father of the bride will be dressed in his tuxedo by this point with his boutonniere on. Typically, only the bride, her dad, and the photographer are present for this sweet reveal. Make sure to have tissues on hand for this one because it's usually very emotional.

Once the reveal with Dad is done and if there's time, we take pictures of the bride with her bridesmaids.

As a side note, most wedding photographers typically bring a second shooter to take photographs of the groom and his groomsmen as they get ready. This could include pictures of them putting on their ties, cufflinks, and boutonnieres.

STAGE FOUR: TO THE CHURCH!

While pre-ceremony shots of the bride and her attendants are underway, I check on transportation to make sure the trolley, limo bus, coach bus, or stretch limo is ready to go. It's up to me to keep an eye on the itinerary and make sure the bride and her entourage take the correct mode of transport on time and trouble free to the ceremony site. I keep the best man's cell number handy and text back and forth with him throughout the day to make sure the groom and his men are on schedule too. Some best men are so organized and efficient I could hire them!

With one assistant at the ceremony site and another at the reception site ahead of time, I also have eyes on the setup and vendors. If any issues arise, I'm made aware right away. Details can be sorted out before anyone else realizes there is a problem. Stress management, Weddings by Allie style.

Once we arrive at the ceremony site, everyone heads to their designated spot as rehearsed and itemized on the itinerary. If there's time, the bride heads into the church for pictures with her bridal party or immediate family—or if scheduled, for her first look photos with the groom. This moves swiftly and ends thirty to forty minutes before the ceremony begins to ensure no one sees the bride before the service. Once photographs are taken, we separate the bride and groom and whisk them into hiding.

When the bride and groom are tucked away, I make sure all the programs are out, check any requested signage, and double-check the unity candle table setup along with anything else the bride envisioned for the ceremony so it's ready to go, exactly as she wanted it.

My past brides tell me the last thirty minutes before the ceremony are the longest thirty minutes of their lives. They wonder if anyone has shown up. Is the music playing? How is the groom holding up? About five minutes before the ceremony begins, I line up the processional and make sure the bride is either with her dad or the maid of honor to help keep her grounded and focused.

Brides should never be left alone. Side note, At one wedding, I noticed that my bride hadn't smiled the entire day. I thought she was simply preoccupied, but minutes before she was about to walk down the aisle, she confessed to me and my assistant that her ex-boyfriend had contacted her the night before. She was obviously conflicted. The wedding carried on, but to this day I'm not sure what happened to her and her marriage. I do hope everything worked out for the best for her whatever that may be.

STEP FIVE: SHOWTIME!

My favorite part of the ceremony is right before showtime when the bride waits behind closed doors with her father or whoever is going to give her away. As majestic music plays, Dad is either in tears or telling jokes or both.

The time has come. The bride is about to walk down the aisle. She draws long, deep breaths as I adjust her veil and dress. I provide a few last-minute tips about how to walk in the dress and reassure her that she'll make it to the altar without any problems. All she needs to do is take her time. In her nervousness, she tells me she forgot everything she practiced at the rehearsal. I remind her that the officiant will talk her through the ceremony. She doesn't have to worry. And then I say, "The next time I see you, you'll be a Missus!"

The trumpets sound, the ushers open the doors, and I hide watching the bride and her dad enter the sanctuary. It's such a great moment to witness. Everything is colorful and vibrant. The scent of flowers fills the air, music vibrates through your bones, and you can sense the electricity of excitement and anticipation in the air. You have a feeling that life will never be the same.

It certainly won't be for the bride and her groom!

Once the bride and her father start walking toward the altar, the officiant will lead them through the ceremony. One of my assistants remains at the church to assist them afterwards, and I head for the reception hall.

Planning Tips

1. Hiring a wedding planner or a wedding coordinator to take care of the background chaos will make it easier for the bride and her mother to relax and enjoy the day.

2. Make sure there is a detailed itinerary for the day to ensure things run smoothly and nothing is forgotten. That list should include everything from when to begin applying makeup and styling hair to where people must be and when. It should have a check list of items and where to take them, including the rings, wedding license, and the bride's change of shoes for the reception.

3. Review pertinent items on the itinerary with the bridal party at the rehearsal to remind them of their roles and responsibilities.

4. Remember that all preparations will likely include photo opportunities.

Secret Confession

SHE WORE BLUE CHIFFON

As an independent wedding planner, I've worked at hundreds of venues from beautiful hotels to country estates and botanical gardens like Houmas House Gardens, as well as museums and historical locations. Baton Rouge has several beautiful historical locations to hold weddings, places like Louisiana's Old State Capitol and one that is particularly special to me, the Old Governor's Mansion.

The Old Governor's Mansion was built in 1930 by Huey Long, a former Governor of Louisiana. Long aspired to be the President of the United States, so he built his mansion to look just like the White House—complete with an oval office and a rose garden! It has a beautiful East Ballroom with marble floors and a stately marble staircase that is perfect for brides to descend with their trains trailing gracefully behind them. I love planning weddings there!

Unfortunately, not everything that happens at the Old Governor's Mansion is as elegant as the building itself. After one particularly beautiful wedding while the bride and groom mingled with their guests during the reception, the caterers alerted me that the elevator was broken. Considering the age of the Old Governor's Mansion, a broken-down elevator was not a shocker, but I knew it had been checked earlier that week. Wondering if the doors might be blocked in some way, I ran down to the basement to check.

Something was blocking the door—or perhaps I should say someone. Dressed in soft, powder blue chiffon, a bridesmaid lay

129

sprawled across the elevator door opening, her legs inside, her torso out. The door repeatedly bumped against her.

As I drew closer, the overpowering odor of vomit hit me. I gagged. The bridesmaid in blue was drunk and had spewed her evening's consumption everywhere. Vomit covered the elevator inside and out, and it covered her too—from her hair to her bare toes. Her chiffon dress was so thoroughly soaked with the stuff that it had become transparent and her undergarments showed right through the fabric.

"Oh my gosh!" I gasped. After I made sure she was still breathing, I ran for help. A couple of the catering staff and the police officer who was running security that night came to the rescue. It was the poor police officer's first night at the Mansion, and I had assured him earlier that nothing exciting ever happened here! Together we managed to carry the vomit-clad, now semi-coherent bridesmaid away from the elevator. Realizing she couldn't stand, we hovered over her, trying to figure out what to do.

Her drunken boyfriend staggered down the stairs and headed toward us. He greeted his girlfriend with kisses on her vomit-speckled face.

I gagged again.

Since she was still unable to stand, we wrapped her up in a blanket like a burrito, lifted her on to a cart, and rolled her into the police officer's car. He was nice enough to take the couple to their hotel. As he got into his car, he turned to me. "I thought you said nothing exciting ever happens here."

I don't think the bride and groom or any of their guests ever found out what happened, and I'm glad for that. Another unexpected situation resolved.

THE RECEPTION

Once the ceremony is over and your pictures are taken—if you're having a post-ceremony photo shoot—some of the pressure surrounding your big day is off. The formalities aren't quite over yet, however. Taking care of them with as little stress as possible requires the same careful planning that went into all the previous elements of your wedding day.

Reception scheduling is probably the single biggest headache for most planners and brides, but after years of managing those kinds of logistics, I have a few tips to share. I'll draw from my experience in Baton Rouge, New Orleans, and most of South Louisiana for examples.

Let's say your venue requires you to supply all your own furniture, dishes, cutlery, food, and so on. If you're planning to use a tent, it may need to be set up two or three days before the wedding. Here in Louisiana where we must always keep an eye on the weather, tents are sometimes set up a week ahead of time to take advantage of the most opportune conditions.

In most cases, vendors begin arriving at the venue for setup around three hours before the reception is scheduled to begin. That may not sound like a lot of time, but keep in mind, experienced vendors have their setup procedures down to a science. They're used to working within that time frame. Extra time will likely cost you extra money.

After the tents are up, the rental company delivering tables, chairs, linens, and lighting will be the next to arrive. Next, the decorator will appear to drape chiffon, hang chandeliers, and place specialty linens on the tables. As the decorator sets the tables, the caterer will begin setting up the food stations and the bar. Then the florist will arrive. You need to make sure the tables and linens are in place before the florist gets there; they can't place flowers on tables that aren't ready. Finally, the band or DJ will arrive.

Once the vendors have completed setup, my assistants arrange all the specialty or personal items in the appropriate places. They'll set up the sign-in table with any special items the bride has requested such as the guest book and pens and a card box. They'll put champagne flutes in place along with cake knives, pictures for a memory table, and favors.

Everyone and everything should be ready at least thirty minutes before the reception is scheduled to begin. That extra half hour is important because guests sometimes show up early. Keep in mind, some caterers and venues begin timing their service the second the first guest arrives. They may not stick around any longer than they have been contracted for, at least without imposing extra charges. That can get sticky. If your reception was supposed to start at seven o'clock in the evening and a guest shows up at six-thirty, you just lost thirty minutes of precious time for your scheduled three-hour reception. Let me tell you, that three hours goes by in a flash! If you want to ensure your reception runs as planned, tell the caterer to not serve until the allotted time.

Most venues are a bit more lenient with time, but always check beforehand. Don't ever assume anything in the wedding world. You may end up with costly surprises, and the last thing a bride needs on her wedding day is an unwanted surprise. Can you imagine showing up to your wedding reception to hear the wedding planner, coordinator, or facility coordinator say, "Well, we now have two-and-a-half hours to get everything done"?

Not good.

LET THE CELEBRATION BEGIN!

When guests begin to arrive, make sure music is playing and the bar is open. With a buffet style reception, the food line should open then too. That way, guests can begin enjoying refreshments. They will be relaxed and ready for the arrival of the bride and groom.

Some venues, caterers, and brides prefer to hold off food service until the bridal party arrives. While this is certainly an option, in my opinion it wastes precious time. It could take thirty to forty-five minutes for the bridal party to arrive after their photography session. During that time, the guests could be eating and settling in. If food isn't served until later, the dance will start later too. Everyone will have to finish eating before the first dance is announced or they will be concentrating on food instead of the bridal couple.

Once the bridal party arrives, I prefer to let the attendants eat and drink with the guests while I whisk the bride and groom away to a quiet spot designated for a private dining moment. Most couples have told me that this was the best decision they made for their reception. That ten to fifteen-minute break gives them a few minutes alone as a married couple and a chance to catch their breath. They're able to share a glass of champagne or a cocktail and enjoy a bite of food before greeting their guests.

One newly married couple grew very relaxed during their private dining session. The bride put her feet up on the table and requested a full bottle of champagne. I checked on them several times, and they kept telling me they weren't quite ready to leave. After about thirty minutes I had to urge them to join their guests!

Before the bride and groom join the reception, I'll set the bride's bustle, remove her veil, and give her a more comfortable pair of shoes to change into if she wishes. She can touch up her makeup too. After a short break and a few moments of calm, the bride and groom are ready to be announced.

If you decide not to take a private dining moment, don't count on a break for the rest of your reception. You'll be swarmed with congratulations and hugs. People will want to take photographs of you and with you. You probably won't have time to eat. If you and your groom have a celebratory glass of alcohol or two without eating, you could easily end up in an unwanted stupor. That's to be avoided. I'm sure you want to remember every wonderful moment of your wedding reception, right?

I strongly recommend that you take a few precious minutes for private dining.

ANNOUNCING YOUR ARRIVAL

Once you're ready to enter the reception, I'll cue the band or the DJ to play your introduction song. Introduction music cues the guests that the announcement is coming and makes sure your entry receives all the attention it deserves.

Some brides choose to have the band or DJ announce the entry of each of their bridal party members as well. If you decide to do this, make sure everyone involved is aware in advance. It's best to have the bridal party enter in the order they did for the ceremony with the bride and groom making their grand entrance last. To make it easier for the announcer to introduce each person, provide a list with each name spelled phonetically. A bit of planning will easily avoid the embarrassment and discourtesy of mispronunciation.

Choose a designated spot for the bridal party to line up in advance. Tell them where to stand when their names are announced and be sure they know how you want them to make their entrance. For example, if you want them to dance into the room and go crazy, make sure they're ready to go all in with the energy and excitement that kind of entrance deserves.

Sometimes the bridal party forms a tunnel with their arms and the bride and groom run through it. If you choose this approach, let them know what to do and where to go after you've run through, so they aren't left standing around awkwardly.

A well-done entry is sure to be captured on camera by a few guests, and it will likely make its rounds on social media. Take the time to make sure that everyone involved knows what they are doing.

ON THE DANCE FLOOR

Once the wedding party has made its entrance and you and your groom have been announced, it's time for the spotlight dance or first dance. If you took professional dance lessons for this, make sure you're well-rehearsed. You don't want to look like robots mouthing the count for each step! You're better off swaying to the music, gazing into each other's eyes, and kissing now and then. A dip at the end of the dance is just the right touch. I promise you, that easy romantic approach is much more effective than a stiff choreographed dance with a bridal couple who looks scared to death.

After the first dance, the bride typically dances with her father. I make sure the bride's father is standing at the edge of the dance floor as the first dance ends, so we don't have to chase around after him. While the bride and her father dance, I lead the groom to his mother, who is waiting by the dance floor. While they wait for their turn, I hand the groom a stiff drink of his choice, like a whiskey neat. Grooms are always grateful for that.

After the bride dances with her father, I hand her a glass of champagne, water, or another drink of her choice. Then the groom and his mom begin their dance. Traditionally, the bridal party dance follows. However, many brides are forgoing this lately claiming it's awkward. So, unless the bridal party has a special choreographed dance to share, we usually open the floor to all guests.

WEDDING CAKE

I always give my brides the option of mingling with their guests for a while or going straight to the cake for cake cutting photographs. Those pictures usually include one with the entire bridal party gathered around the cake table holding champagne glasses. If the bride has an exceptionally large bridal party, I highly suggest doing this sooner rather than later. The later it gets, the more difficult it is to round everyone up. The groomsmen may have removed their jackets and loosened their ties or taken them off altogether. Everyone looks fresher if the pictures are taken sooner.

After the bridal party photos are taken, the best man can give his full toast or offer something short and sweet. Everyone clinks their glasses to toast the bride and groom. Personally, I like to pre-pour the champagne while the groom is dancing with his mom. Then it's ready when the bridal party steps up to the cake table.

A note on champagne; long gone are the days when we allowed the best man to pop the cork. We had too many close calls with the cork, and we don't want anyone to lose an eye or damage the venue. I heard of one wedding where the bride's brother popped the champagne open. The cork flew out of the bottle, hit a chandelier, shattered the glass light bulb inside, and showered broken glass over the buffet table below. Chunks of broken glass glinted across a beautifully dressed whole salmon, and tiny fragments of glass appeared in all the food. Everything had to be thrown away.

We pop the cork for you to avoid that kind of scenario.

Once the toast is done, one of my team or I or perhaps the photographer will excuse the bridal party. That is unless we have ribbon pulls for the bridesmaids.

► **Ribbon Pulls:** If the bride is holding a ribbon pull for the bridesmaids, I round up bridesmaids before the photographer finishes taking pictures.

If you aren't familiar with ribbon pulls, they are small charms placed under the cake with ribbons trailing from them. The bridesmaids or friends of the bride will each tug a ribbon to receive a special prize at the end.

It's helpful to provide a list describing the symbolism behind each charm. I usually tuck it under the cake plateau. When the girls pull the charms, the bride can reference the list to share the significance of what they pulled. Sometimes the bride will choose specific charms for each girl and give them the appropriate ribbon to pull to receive it.

> ► **Cutting the Cake:** The bride and groom cut the cake and place it on a small plate that I placed there ahead of time along with some napkins and two forks.

For some reason, cake cutting is a challenge for most brides and grooms. They look like two deer caught in the headlights! I usually let the photographer coach them on technique because every photographer has a different approach to capturing cake-cutting images. However, I can offer a few tips. Typically, the bride and groom both hold the knife. The groom's hand is on the bottom with the bride's hand resting on top of his. Both of their wedding rings are showing. Together, they slide the knife through the cake twice to cut a small slice, and then they pull the piece out. This is where they lose their minds. It's as if they never have cut a piece of cake before! I step in to pull out the piece they just cut and place it on the plate. I cut it into two small pieces. The couple can decide if they want to feed each other with their fingers or their forks. Either way, it's cute! Then once they feed each other, they kiss. The photographer may decide to take some pictures of the couple holding their champagne glasses.

- ▶ **The Groom's Cake:** The groom's cake is typically cut without as much fanfare. The photographer might capture a few pictures of the groomsmen gathered around the cake as the bride and groom cut it.

- ▶ **Serving the Cake:** By the time formal pictures around the cakes are taken, it's usually about halfway through the reception. At that point, the cakes are cut and served to guests.

A slight problem may arise if different layers of the cake have different flavors and guests request the flavor that happens to be in a layer we haven't cut yet. Of course, I will cut into a new layer if a guest insists. It's just something to keep in mind when you order your cake. If you want multiple flavors, keep the most popular ones in the largest layers.

At this point the couple are finished with most of the evening's formalities, and they are free to dance or mingle with their guests.

ENGAGING YOUR GUESTS

Most weddings provide several opportunities for the bridal couple to mingle with their guests. A few common traditions or activities include the bouquet toss, the garter toss, and the money dance.

The money dance evokes interesting responses. Some people cannot imagine having a wedding reception without a money dance. Others are mortified by the very idea! As with everything else, whether you have one or not is totally up to you. There is no right or wrong way to hold your reception.

A money dance will take some time out of your reception, but it does provide the bridal couple with a semi-formal way of greeting each guest. I recommend creating two dance lines, one for the bride and one for the groom. Give each guest one spin around the room with either the bride or groom. You might bless Grandma with an extra round if she really wants it, but it is best to move things along quickly to avoid getting stuck dancing with Uncle Bob for ten minutes while he shows off his jitter bug moves! Three songs in total are usually plenty to give everyone an opportunity to dance with you.

The bride or her maid of honor will hold a money bag or a basket to collect any gifts. People usually attach money to the groom's suit using the pearl-tipped straight pins that I provide—although if he owns his suit or tuxedo, I don't recommend it. Lately, my grooms have been holding crown royal bags instead. The purple and gold bag works especially well where I'm based because those are the colors for Louisiana State University.

Timing of the money dance is crucial. If you hold it too early, people might not be relaxed enough to jump in. If no one is ready to dance with the bride or groom, everyone will feel awkward. Holding it too late doesn't work well either. Older guests tend to leave earlier, and they'll miss the opportunity to participate. The sweet spot for a money dance falls around cake cutting time, right in the middle of the reception.

Next on the agenda is the garter and bouquet toss. Starting with the garter toss builds some anticipation for the bouquet toss which is usually received with more enthusiasm because of the symbolism involved. Tradition holds that the fellow who catches the garter is the next man to marry. Let's face it. Most guys are not happy about announcing their single status or being pinpointed as the next groom. When the groom begs his single friends to step forward, they tend to line up reluctantly and stand around with their hands in their pockets wishing it were over. The groom slides the garter off his bride's leg, throws it to the guys, and the guys all step back, watching the garter fall to the floor.

UGH! Frustrating, right? I know how to fix this! As the groom slips off his bride's garter, I stand in the wings with a football. I hand it to the groom, and he slips the garter onto the football. He holds out the football with the garter attached. Suddenly it's no longer just a garter. It's a FOOTBALL—with a garter attached—and the game has changed. Now, the single men line up like anxious wide receivers and when the garter—oops, football—is tossed, they dive after it as if the groom threw a long hail Mary pass!

I love that approach. It works every time.

Before the toss, consider whether the bride wants to sit on the best man's lap as the groom removes her garter. If the best man is the groom's father, which happens on occasion, that approach may feel a bit awkward. Be sure to have your wedding planner make a note of this detail on the itinerary, or else the master of ceremonies will automatically invite the best man, the bride, and the groom to come forward for the garter toss. Just another one of the many details that your wedding planner can manage for you on your wedding day.

The bouquet toss ignites a vastly different response than the garter toss. Girls run to the dance floor when the song "Single Ladies" or "Hit Me with Your Best Shot" is playing and the master of ceremonies invites all the single ladies to the dance floor. The girls remove their shoes and hike up their dresses, ready to go. They mean business! The bouquet is tossed on the count of three. Reaching, shoving, and diving ensues. I've seen skinned knees, shredded bouquets, and hair extensions ripped right out of girls' heads. The winner usually takes a picture with the bride before she walks away with the bouquet, victorious.

END THE DAY WITH ELEGANCE

Bringing the reception to a close can be tricky, especially if everyone is having a blast dancing and drinking. I remind my brides that while the reception is a party as far as they are concerned, it's a business for everyone else.

Each of your vendors has an ending time on their contract—the caterer, beverage servers, photographer, videographer, photo booth people, band or DJ, and of course, the venue itself. Most venues will charge a hefty fee if the reception goes fifteen minutes over the time limit. In some cases, venues have charged the bride a thousand dollars for an extra thirty minutes, and that's not including the bar tab.

It's my job to get everyone out on time. That makes me the bad guy and that's okay. I've learned to mentally prepare guests for end of the night. The first step is to announce a last call for alcohol about thirty minutes before the reception concludes. That allows the guests time for one last drink as opposed to rushing the bar when the last song is over and forcing overtime charges with the venue and vendors. Some venues assume the designated end of the evening is the end and won't permit announcing a last call, but if yours will allow it, take advantage of it. About fifteen minutes later, the band or DJ can announce one last song. Often it's their own selection, a traditional song that showcases their talent.

Between those announcements, the bar closing, and the music coming to an end, you'd think guests would realize it's time to leave so the bride and groom can depart, right? I wish it were that easy! Once the band or DJ thanks everyone for coming and asks the guests to head outside for the bridal couple's departure, the wedding planner must be prepared to act. Guests usually don't realize that when a reception goes into overtime, it could cost the bride's parents a pretty penny.

I lead the bride and groom away from reception area and hide them. Then I invite groups of lingering guests to join the happy couple outside for a send-off with sparklers, bubbles, petals or whatever the couple has decided upon. Some guests quickly comply with my request. Others look at me as if I have two heads. How dare I ask them to leave the reception!

If any difficulties arise, I simply send the bride and groom out the door where the cooperative guests are lined up for the farewell. The stragglers will come as the bride and groom run through the lines and jump into their getaway vehicle.

CLEANING UP

While the celebration may be over for the newlyweds and their guests, there is still plenty to do for those of us who are left behind. The next challenge is cleanup.

Early in my career, I learned a treasured lesson from one bride's mother. We were at the Historical Old Governor's Mansion where food is brought in by an outside caterer. In that situation, any leftover food goes home with the bride's parents. At this particular wedding, an overwhelming mountain of leftovers remained. When I showed that mountain to the mother of the bride, she burst into tears and fell to the ground sobbing, "I can't take all this food! I don't have room for it in the car or my refrigerator."

I offered to deliver it to the nearest charity.

That mom's reaction drove home just how emotional and exhausting the wedding day is for the mother of the bride. From that point forward, I decided to help mothers manage the end of the reception. We now have at least three vehicles on hand to deal with these matters. The first is for the bride's specialty items like toasting flutes, cake knives, the guest book, and the bridal portrait. It usually has space for gifts, cards, the wedding gown, and a few other items. The second vehicle is used to transport any extra food and leftover cake to a location with adequate refrigeration. The third vehicle transports decorations and flowers.

Most people forget they own all the floral decorations. If they aren't removed right after the reception, they will be thrown away. What a waste! When there are many arrangements and large centerpieces, sometimes a large SUV or truck is needed to cart them off.

My team and I pack all these items for middle and higher end planning packages. In some cases, I have even delivered them to the bride's parents hotel room. It's gratifying to hand the mother of the bride her room key at the end of the night and say, "Everything is picked up and all the items are in your room." They breathe a sigh of relief and hug me.

Make sure to have a strategic game plan for drawing the reception to a close to avoid chaos and confusion. If you can finish the day on a positive note with great service, everyone leaves with a better memory of the day and goes to sleep happy.

The way an event begins and ends is what people remember most, so plan with care.

Planning Tips

1. Decide ahead of time if you would like a private dining moment with your new husband to unwind, refresh, and prepare for the evening ahead.

2. Make sure your bridal party knows how you want them to enter the reception, in what order, and if there are any special approaches you'd like to take for their entry.

3. To make it easier for the announcer to introduce each person in your bridal party, provide a list with each name spelled phonetically.

4. Review your approach to the first dances to ensure everyone involved is prepared.

5. Tell key people they need to stay near the cake to be ready for photographs and keep the party on track.

6. If you are going to have leftover cake, cut the bottom layer first to keep the top layer or layers intact for easier transporting.

7. Cake cutting should take place roughly at the reception mid-point.

8. If you're planning a money dance, hold it either just before you cut the cake or right after when guests are usually relaxed, enjoying themselves, and ready to participate—before they tire out.

9. Have a strategic game plan for the ending of the reception including where to send any leftovers, flowers, and other personal items to avoid chaos and confusion. Be prepared to politely deal with stragglers.

10. Make sure that whoever is packing up the bridal couple's items labels everything clearly.

11. Remember, the beginning and the end of events stand out most in people's mind, so plan them well.

Secret Confession

SURPRISES, MIKE THE TIGER, AND THE FIFTY-YARD LINE

If there was ever a wedding to remember in my history as a wedding planner, this is it. The bride and groom were huge sports fans who especially loved football. The groom had graduated from Louisiana State University while the bride had graduated from LSU's rival, the University of Florida, where she was once the mascot, Alberta the Gator.

The entire wedding reception was sports-themed from the favors to the wedding cakes. Before the wedding party's arrival was announced at the reception, they put eye black under their eyes— the black athletic tape that the football players wear to block glare. Even the bridesmaids wore eye black. Some members of the wedding party carried footballs. Some wore football helmets.

The DJ introduced each member of the bridal party one by one as they made their appearance to a sports-themed song. They hammed up their entries as if they were ramping up for a game. Some executed football drills, and others launched into end-zone dances like players do when they make touchdowns. Each and every one of them went all out.

At one of our meetings prior to the wedding, the bride informed me that as a surprise for her husband-to-be, she had arranged for an appearance by LSU's mascot, Mike the Tiger. As a football fan myself—and one who adores fun—I was thrilled! Putting Mike the Tiger in a tuxedo vest and top hat for the reception seemed the perfect touch, so I made the arrangements. I couldn't wait to see the surprise on the groom's face.

And then the groom called me. Grooms rarely call unless there is bad news.

"Uh, Allie, I have to tell you. I know Mike the Tiger is coming to our reception."

"No," I said, startled but relieved that he wasn't delivering bad news. "What makes you think that?"

"It doesn't matter, but here's the thing. I'm going to trump Mike the Tiger with a surprise of my own."

"Really? Tell me," I demanded, curious.

"I'm having Alberta the Gator's costume shipped to you. Can you find someone to wear it?"

"Oh my gosh! You bet!" I cried gleefully.

The bride and I decided the most strategic entry point for Mike the Tiger would be after the spotlight dances. Little did she know that once Mike had made his appearance, Alberta the Gator would follow.

The wedding ceremony unfolded flawlessly. The bridal party made their reception entry with eye black and lively antics. I met the mascots in a side room, dressed Mike the Tiger in his vest and top hat, and gave Alberta the Gator a veil and a bouquet.

I cued the DJ. He played the LSU Fight Song and announced Mike the Tiger into the reception. The guests were thrilled! Mike danced and played to the crowd while the groom did a fabulous job of looking surprised.

When Mike completed his show, the music switched to the University of Florida's Fight Song. The bride looked completely confused.

"And now here's Alberta the Gator!" the DJ boomed as the mascot sprang into the ballroom.

The bride almost fell over! The groom got her good.

But that wasn't the end of the fun. What happened next should go down in football history. Mike the Tiger and Alberta the Gator, the mascots for two fiercely rival teams, began dancing together in jitter bug fashion. I will never forget that surreal moment, and I'm grateful for pictures guests took to document it.

Another bridal couple obsessed with LSU football dreamed of holding their ceremony on the 50-yard line at LSU Stadium. They managed to get approval to do so, but because of a sudden change in scheduling the approval was reneged after their plans were well underway. They were determined to make it happen anyway. I was in total agreement. Even if we got in trouble, they would still have a great story to pass on to future generations. Besides, as the saying goes, "it's easier to ask forgiveness than it is to get permission." (And it would make a great story for a book one day—nudge, nudge, wink, wink!)

The plan was to sneak onto the LSU football field after a spring game in April for a "quickie" ceremony just long enough to say, "I do," and take some pictures. The field ceremony would be followed by a full ceremony which had been previously booked at the Amphitheater on LSU campus grounds. Thankfully, permission for that was still in place.

So, what to do? I knew about one entrance to the stadium that was always open. On the day of the wedding, we loaded the bridal party, officiant, and photographer into the buses and circled the stadium several times to make sure the coast was clear of security. We found a window of opportunity and stormed through the entrance to the fifty-yard line. (Folks, please don't do this! In hindsight, I realize how risky it was. We're lucky we didn't get in trouble or fined.) I lined up the bridal party with the bride and groom in front, and the officiant began the ceremony which took all of five minutes. We captured some great photos. Although a few janitors were busy cleaning the stadium, no one seemed bothered by our presence, and we didn't get chased off the field.

TOUCHDOWN!

Man, I love it when dreams come true for my brides and grooms!

We ran off the field and out of the stadium, stopping to take a few more pictures just outside of the stadium where the LSU sign was prominently displayed. It made a great backdrop. Then we went onto the Amphitheater for a beautiful full-length ceremony.

Guess who their ceremony musicians were? Some members of the LSU marching band!

Chalk that one up to another amazing wedding memory.

PHOTOGRAPHS AND VIDEOS

Wedding photography has changed dramatically over the past couple of decades. When I first started my wedding planning business, photographers were still using film. Yep, film. Film is so uncommon now that some of you may not even know what I'm talking about! Way back then, documentary style photography was just beginning to appear. Black and white pictures were considered edgy.

With the rise of digital photos and camera-ready mobile phones, everyone thinks they can be a photographer or videographer. I just posted a wedding photo on Instagram that I had taken with my iPhone. The photographer for that wedding privately messaged me to ask if that was one of his photos. It was that good! I bet he couldn't believe it when told him I took it with my phone.

I may occasionally be able to capture a cool photo, but let's be real. I am not a professional photographer and chances are you aren't either. It takes years of experience, talent, and an artist's eye to capture beauty and raw emotion the way professional wedding photographers do.

Brides, be careful when choosing your photographers and videographers. The old adage, "you get what you pay for" rings as true here as it does with every other aspect of wedding planning. Don't be lured by low prices. Low prices may mean the person you're hiring is inexperienced. They may mean a sacrifice in quality. Long after the cake is eaten, the flowers have faded, and music and dancing are a distant memory, your wedding images will live on. Forever. That's why it's important to choose a talented, experienced professional.

FINDING THE RIGHT PHOTOGRAPHER OR VIDEOGRAPHER

Booking just the right photographer or videographer for your wedding isn't as quick and easy as it might seem. There are several considerations. Although I specifically refer to photographers in the comments that follow, the same considerations apply to choosing a videographer. Please note that some photography businesses offer video services too.

► **Know Who Will Be Behind The Camera:** Sometimes studio owners will charm you with their great personalities and fabulous work but send a third or fourth tier photographer to shoot your wedding day. Meet with the person who will be behind the camera. Review wedding pictures from her or his portfolio, NOT company stock photos. You only get one shot at your wedding photos—no pun intended—so make absolutely certain you are getting what you think you are getting and what you're paying for.

► **Establish Rapport:** Before you book a photographer, meet with several candidates in person to find one you have a great rapport with. After all, the photographer you choose will be coming to your wedding. Just imagine spending eight hours in front of a camera held by someone you can't stand.

Here's another *lagniappe* (a little something extra). Consider recommendations for photographers from your wedding planner. Personally, I have worked with many photographers over the years. Working with photographers whom I've come to know makes everything easier.

I've worked with some photographers hundreds of times. We've worked together so often that we each know how the other works and thinks. We can often guess each other's next moves. For example, I've worked with Warren of Warren Conerly Photography often enough that all he has to do is give me a certain look across a crowded dance floor, and I'll know exactly what he wants from me next.

Now that's teamwork.

It's challenging although not impossible to work with someone new when you don't know how they like to handle things. A wedding day is chaotic enough without trying to figure out on the fly how fast or slow the photographer works, or how to accommodate his or her needs for gathering various groups of people to photograph at the reception. As with all things, however, communication is key. If I haven't worked with a contracted photographer before, I ask a lot of questions before the wedding and on the wedding day. I try to make their job easier to ensure my brides receive the most beautiful, memorable photographs possible.

► **Photographer's Attire:** Make sure that you're clear about your expectations for the photographer's apparel at the wedding. I once had a photographer show up for an outdoor wedding dressed in a casual t-shirt and shorts. I was appalled. Even though we were in Louisiana and it was hot and humid, the wedding was still semi-formal. His attire was not at all appropriate.

WHY VIDEOGRAPHY?

Attitudes toward wedding videos vary. Some of my past brides booked a videographer before they booked any other vendor, while some treated video as an afterthought, only booking a specialist if there was enough money left over in the budget.

Although you probably won't watch your wedding video every night—or even every week—wouldn't it be great to relive it down the road, say on your anniversary? Wouldn't it be wonderful to share your wedding video with your children one day? Wouldn't you love to see your grandparents dancing long after they have gone? Or to revisit memories of the groomsmen launching a dance off in the middle of the floor for the most epic dance war ever?

You can't possibly experience or remember every moment of your reception, but if it was captured on video, you can review it forever. That put things in a different light, doesn't it? One of the saddest statements I ever hear is from a bride who says, "I wish I had my wedding recorded on video." After the wedding, it's too late.

Some brides think that guests taking social media video clips are enough. They aren't. They're short and often blurry with poor sound quality. Yet a professional wedding video doesn't need to have all the bells and whistles or movie-theatre production qualities to be valuable. It could provide hours of raw footage or a ten-minute highlight. Or it could be both.

With video, family members or friends who weren't able to attend your wedding can experience some of it as if they were there. Videographers often upload wedding videos or highlights to various social media sites for easy access.

A good videographer will capture all the emotion and excitement of your day and allow you to relive it over and over again as much or as little as you want.

TIME LIMITS AND SCHEDULING

Videographers and photographers each have time limits on their wedding packages. Make sure you know the timeframes your vendors offer. To explore this idea, let's focus on photographers with the understanding that similar considerations apply to videography.

Most photographers' packages are only six hours long, but these days, albums are composed with a photo journalistic style. They tell the story of the wedding day from start to finish. This approach includes pictures of pre-ceremony festivities, moments like the bride getting her hair and makeup done, bridesmaids getting ready, the groom putting on his cufflinks, and the groomsmen helping the groom adjust his tie. The book usually ends with pictures of the bride and groom leaving the venue and running through two lines of sparklers, glow sticks, or bubbles to their departure vehicle—a Rolls Royce, a Limo, a pedicab or even a horse and carriage.

A six-hour contract with the photographer won't cover all of those precious moments. Brides tend to overlook this important fact. If it isn't in the budget to contract the photographer for an additional hour or two, the bride can either determine what's more important to her: the hair and makeup or the departure picture. Once she makes her decision, we can adjust the photographer's schedule accordingly.

If time is a concern, consider creating a mock departure. Have the guests line up outside before the end of the evening. The bride and groom can run through the line in a mock getaway, the photographer can catch all the juicy moments—like the groom dipping and kissing the bride—and the photographer can leave. The newlyweds and their guests can return the venue and continue the party.

Do check the hours your photographer or videographer is contracted for and plan accordingly. That way, you can achieve the photographic wedding story of your dreams and stay within budget.

A word of caution: when you plan how the day's photography sessions will unfold, schedule all family pictures before the ceremony or immediately after. Don't turn your reception into a family portrait session. Drawing everything to a halt so the band can call the Smith family to the dance floor for a group picture takes something away from the party atmosphere. This may be the only time you have great Aunt Sue, Uncle Billy, and your five-year-old nephew all together and all dressed up, but please, schedule those pictures earlier. Nothing ruins the mood like stopping everything to put the lights on and take pictures.

Nothing captures wedding memories like well-planned pictures and video.

Wedding Planner Tips

1. Choose a photographer with whom you have a good rapport and picture taking will blend seamlessly into the day.

2. See the work of the actual photographer and/or videographer you want to hire to make sure you know what you are getting and paying for.

3. If you can, find a team of vendors who have worked together before, and ideally, photographers who have worked with your wedding planner before. That makes the day flow more smoothly.

4. Ask your photographer how he or she will dress for your wedding, and make sure it meets your standards.

5. Find out how long the photographer intends to be around to make sure he or she will be available to capture all the photos you need—especially if you intend to have a photojournalistic-style album.

6. If having a photographer around for the entire day is beyond your budget, consider staging a departure with the limo before the photographer leaves.

7. If you plan to have a bridal portrait session before the wedding, see the additional tips under the heading, "The Bridal Portrait Session."

THE BRIDAL PORTRAIT SESSION

You may recall that I am originally from Pennsylvania. Hazleton to be exact. It's close to the beautiful Pocono mountains. When I moved to Louisiana and coordinated one of my first weddings there, I came across a strange ritual that I was not familiar with. Apparently, brides in the South schedule what they call a bridal portrait session.

Six to eight weeks before the wedding, the bride has a practice run for her wedding hairstyle and makeup. She steps into her wedding gown and carries a bouquet similar to the one she'll carry on her wedding day and has her portrait taken. The portrait is then ordered in advance of the wedding and displayed at the reception.

At first, I thought this to be a strange custom, but I came to realize its brilliance. Think about it; a bridal portrait session creates a trial run for the wedding day. If the bride is not happy with the way her hair and makeup turn out, she has time to tweak it. If the dress is too loose or too tight, if the hem is too long, or her shoes are killing her, she can tweak them too. I know of a few brides who bought a brand-new wedding gown after the portrait session because they didn't like their appearance in the first.

Brides who choose a pre-wedding portrait session will need to plan carefully. Make sure you schedule an entire day for the portrait session. Yes, it takes that long. If you're employed in a Monday through Friday nine-to-five job, schedule a day off work. Most wedding vendors and venues do not hold portrait sessions on Saturdays because that's typically when they're busy with weddings. Sundays are usually off-limits too. If your vendor isn't enjoying a day of rest, he or she will probably be at a bridal show. Personally, I participate in fourteen bridal shows a year, and all but three of them are on Sundays.

Depending on how your hair is being styled, plan for one to two hours. Makeup application will most likely require an hour. Don't forget to add the time it will take for travel to the portrait session location, twenty to thirty minutes to dress, and one to three hours for the actual photo shoot. Before you know it, an entire eight-hour day is gone.

On top of all that you have to hope and pray the hairdresser, makeup artist, and photographer are all free on the same day. If you plan an outdoor shoot and live anywhere near Louisiana, there's a high chance it will rain. Can you imagine having to reschedule everyone and everything and take another day off work?

To keep things running smoothly, I recommend you do NOT plan to bring twenty people to the photoshoot with you. Beside the photographer and perhaps your wedding planner—depending upon the planning package you choose—just bring your mom and your maid of honor or the mother of the groom. That's it.

I promise, your photographer will thank you for that decision. The more people on the photo shoot, the more chaos. Keep the day as stress free as possible. Surrounding yourself with too many people raises tension, and it will surely show in the pictures. Even though this is a trial run for your appearance on the wedding day, don't underestimate the potential for stress—especially emotional anxiety.

When you are styled to the nines, holding the bouquet, and dressed in your gown with all the accessories including the veil, reality sinks in really quickly. You're getting married! It is really happening. This reality can come as quite a shock to some people. One of my brides breezed through the entire planning process as cool as a cucumber. Then she looked at her gorgeous self in the mirror on portrait day and completely froze.

"What's wrong?" I asked.

"I'm getting married," she replied. "I can't move. Someone hurry and get me a gin and tonic."

I tried not to laugh. Fortunately, the venue had a bar. I brought her that much needed drink. She downed it, and then she was fine.

Here are some useful tips to keep in mind for the bridal portrait session:

1. Take a day off work.

2. Schedule your venue, hair stylist, makeup artist, photographer, and order a smaller version of your bouquet.

3. Wedding gown alterations should be completed before the portrait date.

4. Bring slip-on platform flip flops in case you need to walk over grass or dirt. Grass stains don't come out of fancy silk wedding shoes.

5. Bring water, orange juice, and a healthy snack to keep your energy levels up.

6. Bring a round white or ivory tablecloth to stand on in grass or dirt.

7. Bring a large plastic sheet to stand on in case the ground is damp.

8. Bring a small battery-operated fan, an umbrella, and sunglasses.

9. Once your dress is on, don't touch the sides of the dress. Pick it up from the hemline.

10. Relax and enjoy the day. Think of your groom and smile!

Secret Confession

ONE IN TEN THOUSAND

Some wedding memories might have everything to do with romance, but nothing to do with the bridal couple. Those memories rarely make it to pictures or video. Here's one of those memories, a Secret Confession of my own. I offer it with full disclosure: it's dear to my heart and just a bit embarrassing to share.

As a single mom and professional businesswoman who is constantly at weddings, I conduct myself appropriately and certainly don't go there to find dates, despite the common idea that dates are easy to find at weddings. I do meet a lot of men, however. In twenty-plus years, I have planned and coordinated somewhere around a thousand weddings. Groomsmen average about six for each wedding, ushers four. That means in the course of my career I have encountered approximately ten thousand groomsmen and ushers, most of whom were single. That's without counting the single male guests. When you figure them in, the number of single men I've encountered is staggering.

In all that time, out of all those men, I have only ever dated one. Yep, one. One in ten thousand. Here's the story.

The wedding was located near Brittany Spears' hometown of Kentwood at a beautiful mansion in the middle of nowhere on a sweltering summer day. Pretty typical for a South Louisiana wedding.

The sun was going down, but heat and humidity still hung in the air. Cicadas buzzed loudly and as usual mosquitos were biting. As I set up a display of the bride's accessories, in walked the most attractive man I have ever seen. Tall, dark, and handsome with a killer smile—totally my type. (Even better than Matthew McConaughey from *The Wedding Planner!*) He walked up to me and introduced himself.

"Hi," he said. "My name is Joe. (Not his real name) I'm one of the ushers. Can I help you with anything?"

Swoon. As I had brought no assistants to this wedding, I welcomed his help. He was kind and cordial, a gentleman with exceptional manners. I frantically searched the room for his girlfriend or wife. And as most single women do, I checked his left hand for a wedding ring. No ring. Yes!

But surely that couldn't be right; a guy like this must have a girlfriend.

After we finished placing the bride's items, Joe excused himself and changed into his tuxedo. I slipped into my zone, the place where I get so wrapped up in the moment of the wedding, I forget everything else.

As I lined up the processional in preparation for the ceremony to start, Joe ushered in the guests with kindness and charm. I sent the grandparents down the aisle, then the parents. The bridal party followed. Then came the bride's entrance. The sun shone golden on the mansion, creating the perfect backdrop for a beautiful Southern summer wedding. Joe and I stood side by side in the back behind the guests, watching the ceremony from afar.

Still no sign of a girlfriend or wife.

One moment stands out vividly. As sweat dripped down my back, I asked God why a guy like Joe couldn't ask me out. WHY? I needed a good guy like him in my life.

Abruptly the ceremony ended, and the guests exploded in applause startling me back into reality. The bride and groom kissed and made their exit down the aisle as Mr. and Mrs. It was time to get in the zone again and forget about Joe.

Guests entered the reception area and began eating. I went to set the bride's bustle, and the evening unfolded. Later, as I began to cut and serve the cake, Joe approached me again. He struck up a conversation and we realized we had a mutual love for sushi. He grabbed a piece of cake and returned to the party. A few hours later as the reception wound down, Joe found his way to me once more. By then, I was smitten. A blush warmed my face and we began to flirt a little

In my head I screamed, "Ask me for my number! Please ask me out!"

Some of you may be wondering why I didn't just ask him out. I'm old school when it comes to stuff like that. I prefer the guy to do the chasing and the asking.

Finally, Joe did it. "Would you like to get some sushi sometime?" he asked.

I tried to regain control of my breathing and mustered my response. "I'd love to."

Joe asked for my phone number and as I begin cleaning up after the wedding, he offered a familiar line while he made his exit: "I'll call you."

One week later, no call. Two weeks later, no call. By three weeks, I decided I might as well forget about Joe. But on week four, he finally did call. We had a fabulous date at a fancy Japanese restaurant with the best sushi I have ever tasted. Our conversation was light, flirtatious and fun. He was the perfect gentleman. We shared some Sake and a few lingering gazes across the table. He suggested we go for a walk around a lake, and we did. It was the perfect night; the stars were out, and a slight breeze stirred the air which is rare in South Louisiana.

As we talked and held hands, he stopped and faced me. We had our first kiss under the stars by the lake. I felt as though I were in a movie, a love story, and I was the leading lady. He took me home, walked me to my door, and we kissed goodnight.

Wow! Let me tell you, that went down as one of the best first dates ever.

What happened after that? Well, being the intelligent guy that he was, Joe accepted a great job opportunity up north and moved there within weeks of our first date. He is now happily married and has a child.

How do I know this? We're still friends and stay connected on social media. We almost met up once when I was out his way, but he was away on a business trip and we never connected. Unless he reads this book, he will never know he was my one in ten thousand. I will forever be grateful for the wonderful memories he gave me. Thank you, Joe.

THE INVITATIONS

I nvitations. Ugh! Just the word makes most brides sweat. Why? At first glance, wedding invitations seem pretty straightforward. They aren't. Numerous decisions are required to create the invitation that meets your needs and feels right for you and your groom. It begins with choosing the right card stock, font, color, content, and shape. Then you need to make your guest list and decide how many invitations to order. And let's not forget addressing each one. That's quite a task!

Invitation design has changed a lot since I began my wedding planning career. Invitations used to be quite ornate with lots of shining lilies and flowers framing the card. Purple and fuchsia were the "in" colors at the time. That trend was followed by a shift to clean lines and simple borders—or even borderless—for more refined, elegant look.

Then came the invitation requiring an endless assembly line of construction. A specially designed folder held the invitation, an RSVP card, a reception card, and a map card to help guests find their way to the venues. Silky chiffon bows held the packet together. By the time the packet was assembled and stuffed into an envelope for mailing, postage costs could double or even quadruple compared to regular invitations because of their weight.

When one bride booked every service I offered, she requested I glue a tiny pearl onto each packet cover with a pair of tweezers—and there were three hundred of them! It took me about twenty hours to finish those invitations. After that experience, I added a contract stipulation about invitations. I now make it clear that I won't undertake more than five steps to construct an invitation package. That generally means placing the invitation, reception card, RSVP card, and return envelope into another envelope, and placing that envelope inside a larger envelope that I address and stamp for mailing. These days, as most brides are terribly busy with either school or work, it makes sense for me to prepare the invitations. However, I can't undertake more than the basic steps without an additional fee for my time.

CHOOSING YOUR INVITATION

Ultimately, the style of your invitation is a personal choice. Whether it's funky, eclectic, plain, elegant, or funny comes down to what you like and what you are willing to pay. Invitations help set the tone for your wedding. It may help to keep your overall theme in mind when choosing them.

At that same time, don't be afraid to be original. For example, a wedding set in a cathedral might inspire a certain vision of tradition and elegance. However, if you happen to have two dogs that you love like children and everyone who's coming knows about them, feel free to include a picture of your two dogs on your invitation if you want to. As I said before, it's your wedding. It's what you want that matters.

It's useful to know ahead of time that invitations can be expensive, depending on the features you choose. Some companies charge extra for colored ink. Although it's not a huge cost, colored ink brings an additional fee for each item printed. That means you'll pay extra for each invitation, each RSVP card, each reception card, and so on. The number of text lines the invitation itself can increase price as well. Some invitations limit the number of lines they can hold.

Even the type of printing you choose will impact on your price. Thermography is the classic choice and the one most popular with brides today. After each invitation is printed, while the ink is still wet, a resin powder is sprinkled over the type and heated. Once dry, the print has a slightly raised surface.

Thermography printing evolved from engraving, which was once the only way to have wedding invitations printed. It gives the text a raised surface as well. Still available today, engraving is the most expensive option. The printer constructs a metal plate engraved with your invitation text in reverse. The engraving or recess is filled with ink and then pressed onto the paper one invitation at a time. That's a lot of work which is why engraving is the most expensive process. If you look closely, you'll see that it also offers a crisper, cleaner appearance than an invitation printed with thermography.

Printing features aren't the only hidden costs to wedding invitations. For instance, consider the shape of the card. The post office has a few guidelines regarding the size and shape of an invitation. More postage is required for an invitation with an unusual shape or an invitation that falls outside of the normal range of sizes and dimension. Remember the bows and the tiny pearls I mentioned earlier? Those features create an extra charge too because the bump created by the bow and pearl makes it difficult for the envelope to go through postal machines. The envelopes must be hand-stamped at the post office.

WHO'S COMING?

It's helpful to add a line to your invitation asking your guest to indicate the number of people who'll come with them. That will help determine the right head count for the caterer and for everything else you need to organize. If you're concerned that some people might sneak in a few extra family members, this approach helps to ensure they won't.

Well, usually. One bride I know received an RSVP with ten people added to the number of persons attending. Ten! I advised her to contact that family and let them know that only two people were allocated for their family. This can get sticky if people want to bring their children, especially if you're having an adult-only ceremony and reception. But it's your wedding, and weddings today are expensive.

Most weddings here in South Louisiana take place in the evening at historical locations, museums, and high-end venues. Some people see weddings as a great night out away from the kids. Others are offended if they cannot bring their children along— especially if they had to travel out of state to attend the wedding and have no one around to care for their children.

So, what's a bride to do?

First, a reminder: you cannot please everyone when planning your wedding. Second: decide whether to allow children to attend or not, and stick to your decision regardless of how hard some people may fight you on it. If you decide to have adults only and know some guests may have childcare challenges, consider providing paid childcare for them. If they don't want to take advantage of that service, the decision is theirs. Don't feel badly. They'll get over it.

That sounds harsh, I know. Please, don't get me wrong. I love children. I raised two myself. But sometimes they don't do well at weddings. Have you ever heard a baby start crying just as the bride and groom are about to say their vows? Not good, especially if the person with the baby doesn't immediately get up and take that crying baby out of the church. Now the screaming baby headlines the wedding video that you paid several thousand dollars for, and you can't hear your vows.

Let's not forget the receptions where several kids run circles over the dance floor. Oh yeah, they're having a blast sliding around, bumping into adults who are trying to dance—and their parents are nowhere to be found.

Brides, if you want an adult only reception, stick to your guns. On the other hand, if you want kids at your wedding and you're prepared to accept whatever happens, good for you! Whatever your decision, remember it's your choice and your big day. Have it the way you want it.

WHEN TO MAIL YOUR INVITATIONS

Before you determine your mailing date, before you even print your invitations, determine your "respond by" date. Check with your caterer to find out when they need the final attendance count. Then add a buffer. Typically, that date is at least two weeks before the wedding, but some caterers need to know how many guests you expect three or four weeks before the wedding. If that's the case, set your "respond by" date accordingly.

BEWARE - STRANGE THINGS HAPPEN WITH MAIL!

Make sure to take your fully assembled and stuffed invitation to the post office. Have the post office attendant measure and weigh the envelopes before you purchase postage. DO NOT rely on their self-serve scales in case there is an error. Can you imagine having all the invitations mailed back to you with a red ink message stamped on the envelope: "Insufficient Postage"? What a nightmare!

Once the invitations are mailed, I jokingly tell my brides, "It's a done deal now!"

Secret Confession

MURPHY'S LAW

Two weeks before her wedding, one bride called to tell me that some of her invitations were returned and they were sliced in half.

Sliced in half!

I sent her to the nearest post office to find out what happened. Apparently, the invitations had been run through a post office machine that managed to slice them up. That was the first time I'd ever heard of such a disaster. Unfortunately, the post office could do nothing about it. My bride was frantic. I didn't blame her.

I advised her to gather a team of friends and family members to call each guest. That way, she could determine who had received their invitations and who would be attending. Problem solved.

But that's not the only time Murphy's Law interfered with wedding invitations. Another bride's parents had recently built a new home in a remote area. Invitations were sent out eight weeks before the wedding using their new location for the RSVP return address. As the RSVP deadline approached, no one had responded.

Ten days before the wedding, still no responses had been received. To say I was perplexed was an understatement! I asked the mother of the bride if she had been receiving her regular mail since they moved. Bingo. She was still picking up mail from her old address, but nothing had come to the new address which was on the RSVP envelopes. She went to the post office to investigate. As it turned out, because they had moved to a remote area and the road leading to their home was all gravel, the postman hadn't wanted to deliver their mail!

The RSVPs they'd been waiting for were sitting at the post office the whole time, but no one had ever tried to contact them to let them know the mail was there. Days before the wedding, they had hundreds of RSVPs to go through.

It never ceases to amaze me how many crazy, unthinkable events arise around weddings. You need to watch every step of the process like a hawk. If you pay close attention, however, there are almost always solutions to every problem.

Problem solving is my forte.

YOUR WEDDING DAY, MINUTE BY MINUTE

Now that you've read each section of this book and have some idea of what planning your wedding will entail, let's leap to the end. We'll run through a typical wedding day step by step to give you a rough idea of how your celebration might flow. In this scenario, we'll assume your contracts include everything vendors have to offer.

► 6:00 a.m. You wake up. It's your wedding day! Maybe you'll do a round of yoga, take a run or a luxurious bath. After a nice cup of coffee or tea, your bridesmaids begin arriving to your room, or perhaps they spent the night with you at your Airbnb or home.

- ▶ 8:00 a.m. The hair and makeup people arrive and begin styling your bridesmaids. Halfway through the process, it's your turn to be transformed.

- ▶ 10:00 a.m. Your wedding planner arrives to steam the bridesmaid's dresses and your wedding gown. If you've contracted photographers and videographers to follow your entire day, they'll arrive and begin taking detail shots of your jewelry, shoes, wedding invitation, and specialty items. Usually around this time, your florist and or decorator are working on the ceremony site. The reception venue is opened, and your rentals are arriving along with all the other vendors.

- ▶ 1:00 p.m. As your makeup application and hair styling are underway, the groomsmen have just finished lunch. They're dressing in their tuxedos. The second photographer and videographer are with them taking shots of the men as they adjust their attire, tend to their cuff links, and put on their ties.

- ▶ 3:00 p.m. Hair and makeup are complete. Your bridesmaids pop a bottle of champagne. You toast each other in your cute pajamas or robes and take a quick picture before the bridesmaids and your mom begin getting dressed.

While they are getting ready, you may take a moment to read a note or open a gift from the groom. The photographer and videographer are there to capture that moment.

The wedding planner takes care of any dress issues the bridesmaids or mom may encounter. Safety pins, fabric tape, and a sewing kit may save the day.

Now it's your turn to get dressed. Your mom and wedding planner help you. Once you are finished, you reveal your gown to your bridesmaids, and they ooh and aww in delight. They help you slide on your garter and position your veil.

▶ 4:30 p.m. Your dad is waiting in the wings. He has his tuxedo on, boutonniere in place. All the bridesmaids leave the room and your dad enters. You have a teary, precious moment with your dad. Now it's time for some pictures with your bridesmaids and parents.

The groom and his groomsmen are ready. If they're in the same hotel as you are, they may be in the lobby getting their boutonnieres on. Time for pictures with the groom, groomsmen, and the groom's parents.

▶ 6:00 p.m. The limo bus arrives to take your groom and his entourage to the church. Once they depart, you and your bridesmaids head to the lobby of your hotel. The limo bus has looped around and you're on your way.

▶ 6:30 p.m. You arrive at the church. Although you can't yet see it, the sanctuary is adorned with flowers and candles. The ushers are in place greeting guests and giving each couple a program. Flower girls and ring bearers arrive and look so adorable that people are pinching their cheeks.

▶ 6:40 p.m. Musicians begin playing the prelude music. Guests scurry in and grab their seats.

▶ 6:55 p.m. The wedding planner lines up everyone in the processional.

► 7:00 p.m. Grandparents, parents, and the bridal party begin walking down the aisle in the appointed order. You and your dad wait outside behind the church doors. The faint sound of the organ rises. Your dad tells a couple of his typical dad jokes as he tries to fight back the tears.

Suddenly, the ushers open the doors. The trumpet sounds in a glorious fanfare and all the guests stand. It's your time to walk the aisle toward your soon-to-be husband. Your heart is racing, and you can barely breathe. You see your groom, and all is well. Your dad kisses you. He shakes the groom's hand or hugs him and places your hand in the groom's.

The ceremony begins. It's beautiful and flawless, but it seems to be over in a flash. You are pronounced husband and wife and you kiss. Then you exit the sanctuary followed by your bridal party and family. After stepping outside and circling outside the church, you return to the altar for some quick pictures.

► 8:15 p.m. (Catholic ceremony) The guests proceed to the reception. The reception is all set up with centerpieces in place, candles lit, the lighting held low. The band begins to play, and the bar opens. Hors d'oeuvre are passed around or the buffet line opens for guests to begin eating.

► 8:45 p.m. Back at the church, the photographer is packing up camera equipment. You and your bridal party depart in the limo bus and head to the reception. Your bridal party joins your guests, and you and your new husband retreat to a sequestered area to for a private dining moment, your first as husband and wife. How exciting!

► 8:55 p.m. The wedding planner sets your dress bustle, removes your veil, and gives you a pair of super comfortable shoes to change into for the evening. At this time, you and your groom may toast each other with a cocktail of your choice.

► 9:00 p.m. Once you and your groom are ready to enter the reception, the band announces your entrance as husband and wife. You enter the dance floor and share your first dance as newlyweds. This is followed by a dance with your father. Then your groom dances with his mother.

► 9:15 p.m. After the special dances, you may mingle or go straight to the cake for a few more formalities while guests finish eating. The bridal party surrounds the cake table as champagne is passed for a toast. If you have a large bridal party, things may be a bit chaotic. There's usually one missing groomsman or bridesmaid. Once everyone is rounded up, the bridal party toasts you and your groom.

If you have ribbon pulls for the bridesmaids or friends, they'll draw their souvenirs, and the bridal party will leave. Then you and the groom can cut your cake. The photographer or wedding planner guides you and you and your new husband as you slice the cake, feed each other a piece of it and kiss. Smile for each other—and the camera!

► 9:30 p.m. Now it's time for some fun. You may join your friends and family on the dance floor or mingle with your guests.

- ► 9:45 p.m. Depending on the activities planned, you may stop at some point for a money dance or garter and bouquet toss.

- ► 10:30 p.m. You have about an hour to go for the reception, and the dance floor is full of happily jamming guests.

- ► 11:00 p.m. Around thirty minutes before the end of your celebration, the band announces the last call for alcohol. Your special day is almost over. It flew by! The band plays the last song of the evening, and you enjoy one last dance.

- ► 11:20 p.m. The band invites guests to head to the front of the building for your departure.

- ► 11:30 p.m. The getaway vehicle is in place. The wedding planner has already placed some food to go—like cake and maybe even a bottle of champagne—in the vehicle.

You and your husband run through the cheering crowd, and the photographer takes a few more photos as your vehicle departs. While you head to your destination, your wedding planner begins to break down the wedding décor and puts into action whatever plan you decided upon previously. Items are packed up and organized for transport as agreed upon.

So, you've done it! After months and months of careful planning, a multitude of decisions big and small, lots of joy, and probably a few tears along the way, you're now married to the man of your dreams. Your special day is a precious moment in history, neatly wrapped, full of beautiful moments and memories of a lifetime, and perhaps a few secret confessions of your own.

It's time to begin your happy ever after!

STATES OF EMERGENCY

I had one objective in mind with *Secret Confessions of a Wedding Planner:* to share as much information as possible to help brides make their wedding dreams come true. If you haven't guessed already, I love brides and weddings!

Even as I wrote the final chapter, however, the book didn't feel complete. I'm compelled to share a few more stories that didn't seem to fit neatly anywhere else in the book but held particular relevance while I was finishing it - just as the world was responding to the Covid-19 pandemic.

Over the course of my life and career, I've encountered plenty of uncertainty including several states of emergency that have forced my GPS to recalculate. Each situation has taught me something vitally important about life. With the right attitude, I can get through whatever comes my way. So can you, wedding-wise or otherwise.

HURRICANE KATRINA

In the South we have to deal with torrential downpours, flash flooding, tornado warnings, and sometimes hurricanes. Even if you don't live in Louisiana, you'll probably remember Hurricane Katrina as one of the most devastating storms of our time. My faith in humanity was restored by the incredible response to the disaster and the strong sense of community and connection that emerged.

Hurricane Katrina struck in late August 2005. Although New Orleans and the surrounding areas carried the brunt of the damage, we were affected in Baton Rouge as well. My electricity was out for ten days. I sweat profusely day and night and had to wait in line for water and ice. I had at least ten weddings scheduled through October, all of which were cancelled until further notice, but a calligraphy deadline was approaching for a November wedding in Baton Rouge. With no air conditioning, I would sit on my condo balcony in the early morning when it was cooler and try not to sweat on the envelopes as I addressed each one with care. But that was the extent of my personal suffering. It paled in comparison to what others endured.

After the hurricane, the population of Baton Rouge exploded overnight. Evacuees from areas harder hit than we were poured into our city for shelter. All the hotels were booked solid. The sky buzzed with helicopters carrying the injured to the Pete Maravich Assembly Center at Louisiana State University, which had been turned into a temporary make-shift hospital. A high level of tension and fear permeated the entire city. It felt like a war zone.

We were fortunate, however, compared to New Orleans. I heard stories of bodies floating in the flood waters and watched television reports of stranded people huddling on their rooftops surrounded by water. Those images still haunt me to this day.

There were so many lives lost and so much devastation that it was almost too much to bear.

Once the shock wore off—which took a while—reality set in. Eventually, we began thinking about our lives again and tried to assume some form of normality. And that's when thoughts turned back to weddings.

Across New Orleans and the surrounding areas, many, many brides had lost their homes and their wedding dates. Countless churches and venues in New Orleans had been consumed by flood waters leaving brides with few places to go. The French Quarter of New Orleans was spared, but because it sat like an island in the middle of so much devastation elsewhere it was forced to shut down too.

Churches in Baton Rouge stepped up. For example, to help more couples get married each week, the Catholic Diocese in Baton Rouge temporarily allowed wedding ceremonies to be held on Saturday evenings, something typically permitted in the New Orleans Diocese but not in Baton Rouge. The community of wedding vendors in Baton Rouge rallied together to try to help as many brides and grooms as possible celebrate their nuptials. Vendors donated all kinds of services, from flowers to bridal wear and photography. Bridal shows offered extra prizes for Katrina survivors.

I donated wedding planning services to several brides and tried to help them pick up the pieces of partially planned weddings. I helped them find venues and vendors. I even helped them find wedding gowns donated by my previous brides. Through teamwork, our amazing community of wedding vendors was able to help countless brides realize their dreams.

The year after Katrina, the number of weddings I planned more than doubled to a total of forty-five. To this day, it was the year I planned the most weddings in my career. What a joy to see all those couples marry—a clear sign of hope after such monumental destruction.

WEDDING UNDER ALERT

Fast forward eleven years. I had a Friday night wedding scheduled with a lovely bride on August 12, 2016. The ceremony was to be held at St. Joseph Cathedral. The reception would take place at Louisiana's Old State Capitol, a historical castle-like venue overlooking the Mississippi River.

As the wedding day approached, we watched the weather closely. Although we knew rain was coming, we weren't terribly concerned. Both the ceremony and reception would be held indoors. On the wedding day, heavy monsoon rain poured from the sky.

I arrived at the hotel where the bride and bridesmaids were getting their hair and makeup done. As I began to steam the wedding gown, all of our cell phones exploded with that horrible, blaring amber alert signal. You know the sound; it grabs hold of your chest to make sure you know something bad is hovering. Then flash flood alerts came pouring in. If that wasn't bad enough, the weather reports grew increasingly grim. We were getting too much rain. Far too much rain. Rivers rose so quickly that a state of emergency was declared.

Historical venues like Louisiana's Old State Capitol have certain rules and regulations concerning states of emergency. To find out how we might be affected, I contacted the events director.

"Typically, the building would be closed under emergency situations and all the workers sent home," she told me.

My heart dropped.

"However," she continued, "we aren't affected here so far. If the mother of the bride still wants to hold the wedding, it's her call."

"I'll talk to her and get back to you," I said.

I phoned the facility coordinator at St. Joseph Cathedral and was offered the same council.

When I called the bride and her mother—who just happened to be a previous bridal shop owner—they were both eager to put storm warnings aside and carry on with the wedding. Unfortunately, the storm and flooding kept many guests away, so attendance numbers were low. As the reception began, my assistants received word that some of the roads leading to their homes were closing due to rising water. I sent them home early.

Despite the heavy rainfall and a shortage of guests and assistants, the wedding continued. It was incredible! It certainly met my standard for a successful wedding: the bride, the groom, and their guests filled the dance floor all night long with music and laughter. This couple were brave enough to carry on despite the storm and had an unforgettable time with their families and guests. And the venue stayed dry!

They were fortunate, considering how badly surrounding areas were hit. So much rain fell that drainage systems couldn't accommodate the water. In some areas of Baton Rouge, enough water filled the streets to float kayaks. Less than twenty miles away in Denham Springs, many sections of the city were only accessible by boat!

A couple of days later, my son knocked on my door and told me to look outside. I stepped out on the balcony of my second story condo to discover two feet of water surrounding my building. I scurried down to the first floor to help my neighbor and her dog upstairs to my place as two feet of water filled her entire suite.

Because this storm was given no name, the rest of the nation had no idea about the devastation we endured. It took two years for some people to get back into their homes, and even then, in 2018, a few Federal Emergency Management Agency (FEMA) trailers were still spotted in the area. Still, it makes me smile to know that in the middle of a state of emergency a happy couple got married. My bride had a great attitude. As a result, she had a wedding she and her guests will never forget.

HOPE OVER FEAR

In October 2017, an approaching hurricane threatened another wedding I'd planned. It was scheduled to take place at Oak Alley in Vacherie, fifty miles southeast of Baton Rouge. I didn't meet the bride in person until the night of her rehearsal, but I immediately loved her vibe and her energy, her determination to embrace every moment of life. She was one of the coolest brides I have ever met!

After the rehearsal, I headed back to Baton Rouge. The Oak Alley facility coordinator called me around 8:00 p.m. "We're under a state of emergency," she said. "There's a hurricane approaching. Can you push the ceremony to 2:00 p.m. tomorrow instead of 6:00 p.m. to try and beat the storm?"

My brain whirred. That would be next to impossible since busses weren't scheduled to pick up guests in New Orleans for the trip to Oak Alley until 5:00 p.m.

"You do know we have the right to shut down the entire wedding," the facility coordinator reminded me, interrupting my thoughts.

"Let me see what I can do," I replied. I called the transportation company who could only make a one-hour adjustment. The best I could do was bump up the ceremony to 5:00 p.m. After getting the Oak Valley facility coordinator's permission to go ahead at five instead of two as she'd requested, I contacted the bride to make sure she and her groom were on board and willing to risk a potential hurricane. She had the best attitude ever! "All I need is my groom and the officiant," she said.

Brides, let that be your mantra. Yes, of course it would be devastating if all your plans had to be thrown out because of a hurricane. But in the end, isn't you marrying the love of your life the most important part of the wedding?

I contacted the other vendors who, like me, had an attitude similar to the U.S. Postal Service. "Neither snow nor rain nor heat nor gloom of night" will keep us from showing up at a wedding and performing our duties. We hoped and prayed for the best. The hurricane was heading toward us, but it was still some distance away. Hurricanes are fickle and at any moment, they can shift course. Many times, we gear up for a major hurricane only to find it suddenly turn and head toward Texas, Alabama, or Florida instead.

Unfortunately, the officiant threw a kink into our plans. Through a series of text messages, she told me that she would not drive to Oak Alley under a state of emergency—even though it is totally legal to drive under those conditions if you're doing it for work. I suspected she was still skittish from everything that had happened during Hurricane Katrina. Many people were.

Although I had my own license to perform weddings—I got it just in case something like this should ever happen—I preferred to focus on the wedding details and caring for the bride. Fortunately, because of my connections I managed to find a replacement.

When the wedding day arrived, we were still under a state of emergency, the sky overcast with light rain. The groom was worried.

"I think we should cancel the reception," he said.

I looked at the sky and the lightly falling rain. "You know Louisiana weather. We might not even see the hurricane. Why not go ahead with the reception? If the weather holds, you'll always regret the decision to not celebrate your wedding."

"Okay," the groom said. "You're right."

Because the rain remained light, we decided to hold the ceremony on the balcony of the mansion at Oak Alley which faced a grand driveway of majestic oaks. (If you Google "Oak Alley," you'll see the magnificent sight that provided a backdrop for the bride and groom as they said their vows.) As the reception began, we received word that the hurricane's path had slightly shifted to the northeast, toward Mississippi. I felt sorry for Mississippi, but we were grateful!

The reception at Oak Alley met my wedding success gauge with a full dance floor, lots of laughter, and a clearly happy couple. The bride and groom had a truly memorable day. Sometimes dreams really do come true—especially when you choose hope over fear.

THE CHOICE IS YOURS

Life throws curve balls at the most unexpected times. Whether it involves your wedding, your job, your family, or some other circumstance, plans will be disrupted. I think of my Oak Alley bride and her incredible attitude. Choose hope over fear. Whether you go ahead with your plans, revise them, or put them on hold, it's matter of deciding what you can live with and what you can live without, and then stepping boldly into your future.

A NOTE OF GRATITUDE

Dear Readers,

As the writing of this book draws to a close, I am filled with an overwhelming feeling of gratitude.

I am thankful I took a leap of faith and ventured out to start my own business all those years ago, even though I was scared to death.

I am thankful that God and the Universe gave me the strength to persevere as a single mom entrepreneur. It brought so many blessings! Being a sole proprietor allowed me to call the shots, and it gave me the freedom to be home with my kids when they needed me.

I am thankful for the work provided to me by the wedding and event industry, and for the hundreds of wedding vendors and professionals I have the honor of working with side by side on a regular basis. I am in awe of your talents and love our comradery!

I am grateful for all my brides and grooms, past and present, for their families and bridal parties. What wonderful moments we have shared over the years!

I am thankful that my reputation gave me a voice and a platform for teaching and inspiring others to start their own wedding planning businesses. It's exciting to watch these people who have become friends grow in the wedding industry and experience amazing changes in their lives.

I am thankful I acted on my dream to write a book for brides and anyone who loves weddings. I hope it provides the right amount of advice, guidance, and a little bit of levity to help you get through the wedding planning process.

I am grateful for my children, family, and friends who have supported me and loved me through this book project and everything else I've undertaken.

And finally, I am grateful to all the readers who took the time to read through these pages. Thank you, each of you!

If any of you have questions or want to reach out to me for any reason, I'm here for you. You can find me on all social media sites as @weddingsbyallie and my website at www.weddingsbyalliellc. com. Message me any time. I'd love to hear from you.

Wishing each of you abundance and love,

Allie

Baton Rouge, Louisiana

June 2020

ACKNOWLEDGEMENTS

Writing a book was far more difficult than I anticipated. I always believed that everyone has a book inside of them, but now I know why not everyone gets around to writing it. The process is challenging to say the least, and it takes a team—no, a village—to create even a small book like this one.

I could not conclude *Secret Confessions of a Wedding Planner* without thanking some very special people in my life. Some contributed to the ideas contained in this book, some worked on it with me, some supported and encouraged me throughout its creation, and some inspired me to dig my heels in and get it done! There are many people to thank, and I apologize in advance if I forget anyone.

First and foremost, I want to thank my daughter, Briel. She is my biggest supporter, not just with this project but in my life. Without her cheering me on from the sidelines, I would not have made it. Thank you, honey, for your advice, for lending an ear when I vented my frustrations, ready to change my mind and toss it all away. I'm so grateful for your love and encouraging words. Thank you for agreeing to be the beautiful model on the cover of this book! *Secret Confessions* is for you. I love you with my whole heart and soul.

Great appreciation also goes to Warren and Miranda Conerly, the wedding photographers who shot the cover of this book. You have become my family.

I also want to thank my best friend, my accountability partner of twenty years, Jeanne Gremillion. Your support and encouragement led to the actual writing of this book, and I am forever grateful for your friendship.

When I wasn't sure how to begin writing or how to keep going, Nanette Saylor coached me in the beginning stages and held me accountable to the progress of the book. A big thank you to her too!

Many wonderful vendors have become my friends over the years. I'm grateful to them for their support of my business and my school, the WBA School of Planning & Event Institute: Helen Durham of Gabrielle's Bride and Occasion Salon, Milissa Duhe of Designs by Milissa, Donna Devall of Tie the Knot Chapel, Jeff Vance of Surf Vibes, James Dunnegan of Party Portraits Photo Booth, Janine Thibodaux of Houmas House Estate, and singer and musician Michael Liuzza. A big, grateful shout out to Billie Menard of *Weddings with Style Magazine* and Malcolm Anderson for being great Bridal Expo partners.

Thank you to those who contributed comments to the book: Milissa Duhe, Sarah Corie of Eye Dew Weddings, Caryn Roland of Heirloom Cuisine, Rewind Band, and Janine Thibodaux.

I am exceedingly grateful to the members of my team at the WBA Bridal Consultants Association: Vice President Ramona Tauzin, Secretary Sarah Corie, and head coordinators, Jill Swindle, Chris Keller, and Veronica Mosgrove. To all the current team members who assist me, feet on the ground: Aaron Sanchez, Angel Williams, Bianca Rogers, Brianna Brady, Carrie Smith, Carolyn Smith, Cyne' Badeaux, Deanna Johnson, Deborah Shaler, Huong

Hoang, Jailyan Badeaux, Karen Hayden, Kathleen Watson, Kearia White, Marvette Thomas, Michelle Charlot, Paige Lute, Paola De Diego, Shineka Hogan, and Teri Jeannsone. You all are the most incredible, hardworking, brilliant group of ladies that I know. Thank you for your continued support and loyalty. I could not do all that I do without you!

To my editors, Sophie Bennett, who got this book rolling, and Deborah Froese who put her final golden touches on this book. Deborah, you have been so wonderful to work with and due to your magic, this book flows perfectly! You made me sound like a true writer! Thank you for all you did to make these pages all that they are.

Thank you to the fabulous Kate Butler with Kate Butler Books and Inspired Impact Publishing. I was so blessed when we connected at Jack Canfield's Breakthrough to Success Conference. This book would not be in existence without you.

A special thank you goes to Colin Cowie, celebrity wedding planner, who was my very first wedding mentor. I admire him greatly, and I have always aspired to be like him!

David Tutera, thank you so much for writing such a beautiful and gracious forward. I have always been a huge fan of David's. We've met several times over the years. Spending a short time working with him at a bridal show allowed me to get to know him more on a personal level and appreciate what a beautiful soul he really is! I love you David!

Several other people didn't contribute directly to this book but have inspired me beyond belief. Even though I met each of you only briefly, your impact on my life has made me who I am today. First, to my very first mentor, Tony Robbins. Tony, you have been the most influential person in my life. Discovering you late one night after the passing of my father changed the trajectory of my life. You were the one who inspired me to start my wedding planning school. Listening to your teachings gave me the tools I needed to build my business as a single mom. Attending Unleash the Power Within with you in Orlando and doing the "fire walk" made me realize nothing can hold me back. Meeting you in Phoenix was a highlight.

In 2016, when you were on the Home Shopping Network, I called in with a testimony about how you helped change my life. By a miracle, I was able to speak to you directly and share all the ways you inspired me. Then you blessed me with a chance to attend your $10,000 Business Mastery Seminar—a seminar that had been on my vision board for five years! I am forever grateful.

I also want to thank Jack Canfield whom I discovered through the movie "The Secret." With his incredible wisdom and Zen-like nature, he has been the teacher of my life. When I attended Jack's One Day to Greatness seminar in 2016, he ignited a fire in me. I knew I had to finally finish this book. Attending his 2019 Breakthrough to Success seminar gave me the connections I needed to make *Secret Confessions* a reality.

My most recent mentor, Lewis Howes, deserves a big thank you too. Lewis has taught me more about branding and social media in the last three years than I have learned in my entire life! After attending his amazing Summit of Greatness seminar in Ohio, I feel like I found my "tribe." His humble nature and generous soul have inspired me to, as he says, "Do something great!" Thank you, Lewis, from the bottom of my heart. I appreciate you greatly.

I'd also like to thank my parents, Hildegarde Lapcoskie and Albert Lapcoskie. Even though they are no longer with me, their spirit of love is felt every day. They supported me, loved me always, and shaped me into who I am today.

And last but not least, to all of my students who have attended my WBA School of Planning and Event Institute: thank you for your support! To all of my wonderful, beautiful, past brides: you are the true inspiration for this book. Thank you to my present brides who keep me going, and my future brides who give me hope! I love you all.

BIOGRAPHY

For more than twenty years, Allie Wester has brought resourcefulness, tenacity, and good humor to her role as a professional wedding and event planner. From organizing major events such as Baton Rouge's largest outside concert event, Live After Five, and Miss USA parties to producing hundreds of bridal trade and fashion shows and coordinating more than a thousand weddings and events, Allie is considered South Louisiana's top wedding and event expert.

In 2004 she created the WBA School of Planning & Event Institute to train others how to start their own wedding and event planning businesses. Since that time, she has taught and inspired over 1,100 students.

Allie is also a single mom of the two most amazing young adults on the planet, Briel and John Michael. For more information, follow me on all social media channels @weddingsbyallie or you can email weddingsbyallie@yahoo.com.

www.ingramcontent.com/pod-product-compliance
Lightning Source LLC
Chambersburg PA
CBHW070914130626
46555CB00001B/134